Fortress • 30

Fort Eben Emael

The key to Hitler's victory in the West

Simon Dunstan • Illustrated by Hugh Johnson

Series editors Marcus Cowper and Nikolai Bogdanovic

First published in Great Britain in 2005 by Osprey Publishing,
Midland House, West Way, Botley, Oxford OX2 0PH, UK
443 Park Avenue South, New York, NY 10016, USA

Email: info@ospreypublishing.com

A CIP catalogue record for this book is available from the British Library

ISBN 1 84176 821 9

Editorial by Ilios Publishing Ltd (www.iliospublishng.com)
Design: Ken Vail Graphic Design, Cambridge, UK
Index by Alison Worthington
Maps by The Map Studio Ltd
Originated by The Electronic Page Company, Cwmbran, UK
Printed in China through World Print Ltd.

05 06 07 08 09 10 9 8 7 6 5 4 3 2 1

For a catalogue of all books published by Osprey Military and Aviation please contact:

NORTH AMERICA
Osprey Direct, 2427 Bond Street, University Park, IL 60466, USA
E-mail: info@ospreydirectusa.com

ALL OTHER REGIONS
Osprey Direct UK, P.O. Box 140 Wellingborough, Northants, NN8 2FA, UK
E-mail: info@ospreydirect.co.uk

www.ospreypublishing.com

Dedication

To Nick and Ronald without whom this book would never have seen the light of day.

Artist's note

Readers may care to note that the original paintings from which the colour plates in this book were prepared are available for private sale. All reproduction copyright whatsoever is retained by the Publishers. All enquiries should be addressed to:

Hugh Johnson, Upper Flat, 218a Station Road, Edgware, Middlesex, HA18 8AR, UK

The Publishers regret that they can enter into no correspondence upon this matter.

Acknowledgements

Belgian Army Museum Brussels; Nick Cuyvers; Kurt Engelmann; Fort Eben Emael; Charles B. MacDonald Office of the Chief of Military History Department of the Army; National Archives and Records Administration; Ronald Pawly; Photo Centre de Documentation historiques des Forces armées; Len Shurtleff, Great War Society; Joost Vaesen. Colour photographs by Simon Dunstan.

The Fortress Study Group (FSG)

The object of the FSG is to advance the education of the public in the study of all aspects of fortifications and their armaments, especially works constructed to mount or resist artillery. The FSG holds an annual conference in September over a long weekend with visits and evening lectures, an annual tour abroad lasting about eight days, and an annual Members' Day.

The FSG journal *FORT* is published annually, and its newsletter *Casemate* is published three times a year. Membership is international. For further details, please contact:

The Secretary, c/o 6 Lanark Place, London W9 1BS, UK

Contents

Introduction

The Brialmont forts

Following the Franco-Prussian War of 1870–71, the Belgian government undertook a comprehensive review of the country's defences against the threats posed by both the German Empire and the French Republic. Static field fortifications were much in vogue across Europe in the late 19th century, despite the emergence of evermore powerful and accurate artillery weapons. Only the city of Antwerp featured any modern fortifications, built in response to the threat posed by Napoleon III in 1859. The Belgian engineer Général Henri Alexis Brialmont was tasked with updating the defences of Antwerp and creating a ring of forts around the cities of Liège and Namur that lay astride the natural invasion routes from the east and west. These were completed by 1890, with Liège surrounded by a ring of 12 forts[1] and Namur by nine.

The Brialmont forts were of modular design made up of four basic elements: a gorge front, a central redoubt connected by a gallery to a counterscarp coffer. The whole structure was landscaped into the surrounding terrain, thus presenting a much lower profile to direct fire weapons. The central redoubt incorporated the ammunition magazines and the fort's principal weapons, which were large-calibre guns, ranging from 120mm and 150mm to 210mm howitzers, located in retractable armoured steel cupolas. Therein lay one of the fundamental design flaws of the Brialmont forts, whereby all the major weapons were concentrated in the central redoubt with their high explosives magazines nearby. This was compounded by the use of inferior concrete and construction techniques that weakened the overall integrity of the structure. Furthermore, the two fortress rings of Liège and Namur were not mutually supporting, and neither were several individual forts within each ring. None of the forts was modernized between 1890 and the outbreak of war in 1914. Général Brialmont also proposed a fortress to cover the approaches to the town of Visé, north of Liège, but this was declined by the Belgian government[2]. It was to be the invasion route of the German First Army in August 1914.

The Schlieffen Plan

In November 1913, Belgium reaffirmed her status of neutrality that had been guaranteed by the Great Powers since it was first declared in 1839. These countries included Great Britain and Prussia, which was superseded in 1871 by the German Empire. In the first years of the 20th century, the latter's economic and military strength grew at a prodigious rate, threatening the stability of Europe. As early as 1905, the Chief of the Great General Staff, Graf Alfred von Schlieffen, devised an operational plan for the defeat of France. In the event of a simultaneous war against both France and Russia, the Schlieffen Plan advocated a pre-emptive strike against France before the unwieldy Russian Army had time to mobilize fully. As the French were determined to recapture the lost provinces of Alsace and Lorraine in time of war with their much-heralded Plan XVII, Schlieffen determined that

[1] The 12 Liège forts comprised six on the eastern side of the Meuse River with, from north to south, Fort Barchon, Fort Evegnée, Fort Fleron, Fort Chaudfontaine, Fort Embourg and Fort Boucelles, while on the western side were, from north to south, Fort Pontisse, Fort Liers, Fort Lantin, Fort Loncin, Fort Hollogne and Fort Flemalle. The forts contained a total of 400 heavy-calibre weapons with a garrison of approximately 500 men per fort. The perimeter of the fortress ring was 52km with the average distance between the forts being 1,900m and the largest gap being 6,400m between the forst of Boucelles and Embourg.

[2] On hearing the decision, Général Brialmont declared – 'Vous pleurerez des larmes de sang pour n'avoir pas construit ce fort' – 'You will shed tears of blood for not building this fort'.

the bulk of the German Army should attack through Holland and Belgium and envelop Paris from the north-east as the French Army advanced into Alsace and Lorraine. Only screening forces were to hold the line in the two disputed provinces and along the borders of Prussia and Russia to the east. Little consideration was given to Dutch or Belgian neutrality as the German High Command presumed that the French would be equally dismissive of such diplomatic niceties and advance their own forces to the Meuse River at the outbreak of war[3]. Once France was defeated, the German Army would be redeployed to the eastern front to confront the Russians. Fundamental to the whole Schlieffen Plan was that the vast majority of the German Army be committed to the concerted attack through Holland and Belgium and into northern France. The ratio of forces for this attack as against troops on other fronts was deemed to be 9:1. On his deathbed in 1913, Graf von Schlieffen was reputed to have demanded 'Keep the right wing strong!'

Following the outbreak of World War I on 4 August 1914, the Brialmont forts surrounding Liège were reduced one by one by the systematic bombardment of 21cm Skoda mortars and 42cm Krupp 'Big Bertha' heavy howitzers. Fort Loncin on the western side of Liège held out until 15 August, when a German round penetrated the main ammunition magazine, causing a catastrophic explosion that entombed half of the fort's garrison of 550 men – arguably the result of basic design flaws and inadequate construction techniques. Fort Loncin was never rebuilt after the armistice, and it remains a memorial to the Belgian dead of World War I and the gallant defenders of Liège. The Belgian forts built during the 1930s were designed to withstand attack from heavy siege artillery and none fell to conventional assault, although Fort Battice suffered heavy casualties when Bunker I exploded. (National Archives and Records Administration)

Between its formulation in 1905 and the outbreak of war in 1914, the Schlieffen Plan was modified by General Helmuth Moltke, Schlieffen's successor as Chief of the Great General Staff, with the fine tuning left to the dour and humourless General Erich von Ludendorff, who in the best traditions of the Prussian military caste believed that peace was merely an inconvenient interval between wars. The plan now called for stronger forces in Alsace and Lorraine as well as Prussia, thus weakening the right wing that was to attack through Belgium and Luxembourg, but not Holland. The main axis of the assault was now directed over the rolling plains north of Liège, with the city itself to be captured by a coup de main as its railway facilities were vital to sustain the German advance and had to be taken undamaged. By August 1914, five German armies (First to Fifth) were poised to attack through Belgium and Luxembourg with a further two armies (Sixth and Seventh) forming the left wing. The original Schlieffen Plan had called for just two corps. Only time would tell whether the right wing had been fatally weakened.

The battle of Liège

On 2 August 1914, Germany delivered an ultimatum to the Belgian government demanding free passage for the German Army through Belgium and on to France. When this was denied, the German Army invaded Belgium two days later. As a guarantor of Belgian neutrality, Great Britain declared war on Germany on the following day and immediately despatched the British Expeditionary Force (BEF) to the beleaguered country. On the same day, General Carl von Bulow's Second Army began its assault on the city of Liège in the first battle of the World War I. The attack by 30,000 men under General Emmich suffered heavy casualties from the defending forts and the assault faltered. General Ludendorff, who had returned to the colours in July 1914, assumed command and resumed the offensive with Zeppelin raids against the city to terrorize the populace while he personally led the 14th Brigade through the largest gap between the forts where the supporting fire was at its weakest. The city fell on 7 August, but the surrounding forts remained unvanquished

[3] The German Imperial Chancellor, Dr. Theobald von Bethmann-Hollweg, famously dismissed the 1839 Belgian neutrality act as 'a scrap of paper', and it was for 'a scrap of paper' that the British Empire went to war in 1914.

and capable of interdicting German supply lines into Belgium. It was essential that they be captured or destroyed.

Siege artillery was demanded directly from the Krupp works in Essen. On 12 August, two massive 42cm howitzers, nicknamed 'Dicke Bertha', arrived outside Liège and were assembled prior to the onslaught. The heavy howitzer was capable of firing a projectile weighing over 775kg (1,700lb) and the first target was Fort Pontisse threatening the advance of General Alexander von Kluck's First Army to the north. At 1830hrs, the first ranging shell was fired at the fort. The report was heard over 5km away in the heart of the city. Other rounds followed until they found their mark. The fort was pummelled to destruction. One by one the forts were destroyed with methodical precision. The defenders suffered untold hardship as the ventilation systems failed and the gun emplacements collapsed around their heads. By 15 August, only the forts of Flemalle and Hologne remained intact. A German delegation approached the forts to discuss surrender terms. The Belgian commanders were advised to see the destruction wrought on the other forts to forestall further futile bloodshed. The defenders refused and the merciless bombardment continued throughout the day. At 0730hrs on 16 August, the final position surrendered. The battle of Liège was over[4].

On the following day, the victorious German Second Army, together with the First and Third, continued the advance, forcing the remnants of the Belgium Army back towards Antwerp. The capital, Brussels, was captured on 20 August. However, the rigid timetable of the Schlieffen Plan had been severely compromised by the determined Belgian resistance. The arrival of the BEF at Mons caused further setbacks to the plan, and it faltered irretrievably on the Marne River. A portion of Belgium around Ypres remained in Allied hands. There followed four years of bitter trench warfare, with all sides suffering horrendous losses. Of the 267,000 men mobilized into the Belgian army, 13,716 were listed as dead with 44,686 wounded and 34,659 as prisoners of war or missing in action – a casualty rate of almost 35 per cent. Another 50,000 Belgians died during the oppressive German occupation that only ended with the Armistice on 11 November 1918.

The Versailles Treaty

There were many military lessons to be drawn from World War I. By 1917, the Allies had developed sophisticated combined-arms tactics employing artillery, aeroplanes, tanks and infantry in coordinated attacks that, by the end of 1918, had battered the German Army into submission. But the cost was beyond measure. Rapid demobilization quickly led to the loss of such capabilities and expertise. It had been the war to end wars, and any repetition was inconceivable. To many, the power of the defence now so outweighed that of the offensive arms that attack was futile. To the French, the answer lay in a refinement of the field fortifications that had proved so effective during the Great War. Marshals Ferdinand Foch, Henri Philippe Pétain and Général Joseph Joffre favoured such a scheme. As the saviours of France in World War I, there were few who would argue against them. In January 1930, the Minister of War and former Minister of Veterans Affairs, André Maginot, proposed that a powerful line of fortresses be built from Switzerland to the Ardennes and from the Alps to the Mediterranean Sea barring any invasion from the east. See Osprey Fortress 10: *The Maginot Line 1928–45* by William Allcorn (Osprey Publishing Ltd: Oxford, 2003)

Named the Maginot Line, construction was undertaken in five phases during the 1930s. Most of the forts were deep underground and thus

[4] The psychological effect on the Allies of the destruction of the Liège forts was considerable, leading the French to remove many artillery pieces from their static fortresses that were now deemed to be too vulnerable. These included those from Forts Douaumont, Souville and Vaux with almost catastrophic consequences during the Battle of Verdun in 1916. See Osprey Campaign 93: *Verdun 1916* by William Martin (Osprey Publishing Ltd: Oxford, 2001)

impervious to conventional artillery fire with interconnecting tunnels stretching for scores of kilometres. Thousands of men lived subterranean lives for months at a time to service the Maginot Line's formidable array of artillery weapons and machine guns. The line stretched as far as the Ardennes Forest. which the French believed to be impassable to conventional forces. Similarly, the line did not extend along the Franco-Belgian border, although a very basic string of pillboxes and strongpoints was later built along the frontier. The construction of such massive fortifications consumed a large percentage of the defence budget, but more significantly it gave rise to a belief that the Maginot Line was impregnable against conventional assault. Furthermore, funds were diverted from the creation of modern mechanized forces as advocated by younger officers, such as Colonel Charles de Gaulle. Tanks remained subordinate to the infantry as they had been during World War I. Worst of all, it engendered a mentality of positional warfare among the French High Command that infected the Belgian Army as well.

The other victors of World War I drew different conclusions from the French, beyond the common desire not to repeat the slaughter in the trenches.

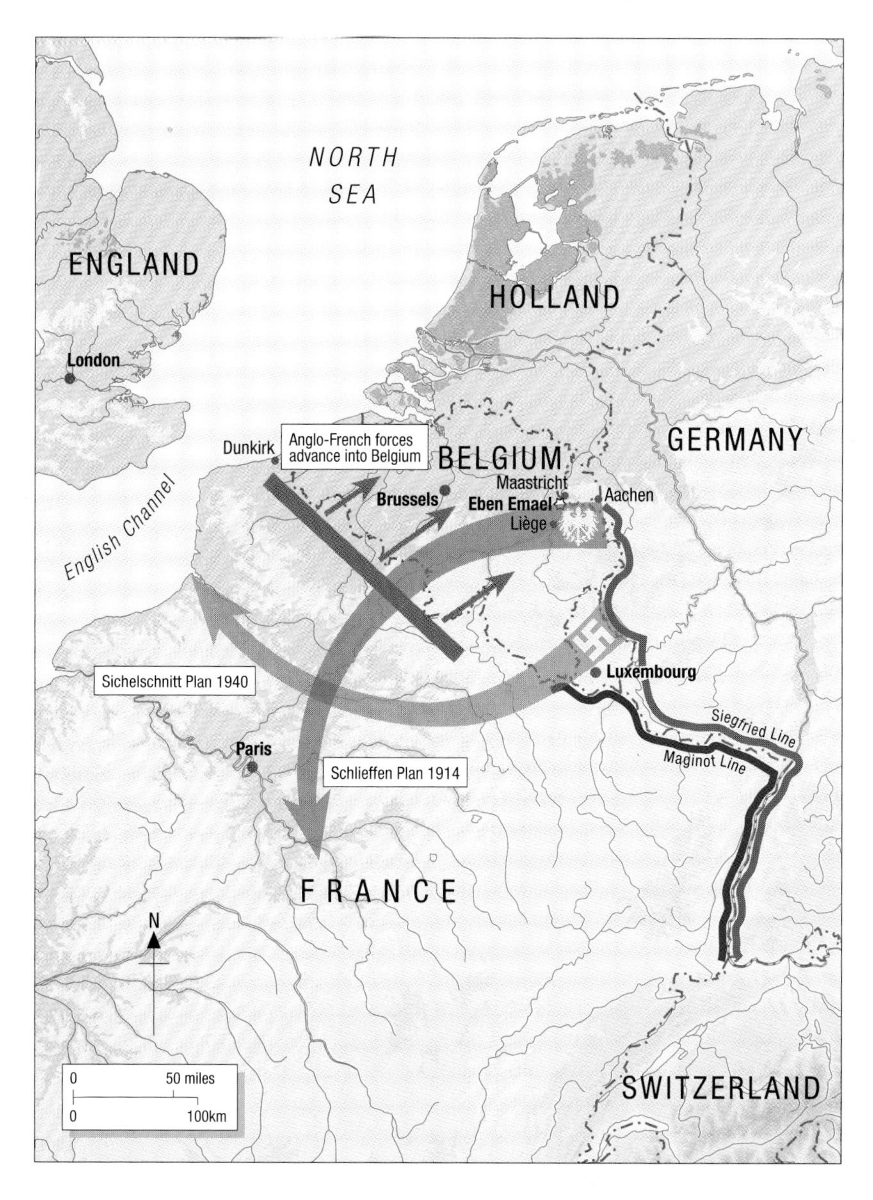

The Schlieffen Plan of 1914 was designed to envelop Paris from the north-east, but determined resistance from the Belgian, British and French armies disrupted the strategy and it faltered on the Marne and Yser Rivers resulting in four years of ghastly trench warfare. In 1940, the Germans lured the British and French mobile forces into Belgium. They then unleashed the 'Sichelschnitt' or 'sweep of the scythe' to split the Allied armies and precipitate the fall of France in just 42 days. (© Osprey Publishing Ltd)

Britain retreated behind her bastion of the English Channel, her most effective fortification line, and her forward defence of the Royal Navy. Eventually, with war clouds in Europe looming once more, Britain embarked on the creation of a strategic bomber force that would allow her to strike at her enemies without recourse to the commitment of ground troops on the Continent. In the 1930s, there was a belief that 'the bomber will always get through' to wreak havoc on the enemy as shown to devastating effect during the Spanish Civil War of 1936–39. The British promptly negated their own argument by inventing radar. To America, any future conflict in Europe became anathema and she withdrew into a self-imposed period of 'isolationism' that effectively emasculated the ability of any international body like the League of Nations to constrain expansionist powers such as Fascist Italy and Imperial Japan. The common denominator of all the victors of World War I was that none was prepared mentally or materially for the next war.

By the terms of the Versailles Treaty of 1919, Germany was made to pay dearly for her war of aggression between 1914 and 1918 – the French demanding 'L'Allemagne paiera!' – 'Germany will pay!' – through reparations. Parts of the Rhineland were occupied and other economic assets were appropriated. The German army was reduced to 100,000 volunteers, and much of the High Seas Fleet, as well as all 150 submarines, was seized by the Royal Navy. Over a third of the army's artillery, some 5,000 pieces and 25,000 machine guns, was surrendered to the Allies. It signalled a humiliating defeat for the German people. Many veterans of the war felt that the German Army had not been defeated by force of arms but had been betrayed by deceitful politicians at home. The myth that the German Army had been 'stabbed in the back' was born. It was a recipe for resentment and revenge; embodied in the figure of Adolf Hitler.

Position Fortifiée de Liège

As one of the victorious Allies, Belgium received a proportion of the war booty, including many of the aforementioned artillery weapons and machine guns. On 7 September 1920, France and Belgium signed a defensive pact, transforming their temporary wartime alliance of necessity into a lasting treaty. In 1923, after Germany failed to deliver reparation shipments on schedule, Belgian troops joined the French army in the occupation of the *Ruhrgebiet*. However, they encountered determined passive resistance and the occupying troops gradually withdrew from the Rhineland over the coming years. It was a portent of the resurgence of the German nation, compounded by the rise to power of the Nazi party in 1933. Once more the threat from the east became apparent to the Belgian government and once more it undertook a comprehensive review of the nation's defences.

With the economy shattered by the war and the brutal German occupation, Belgium was in no position to lavish large quantities of public money on defence, ranging from 11.23 per cent in 1921 to just 3.73 per cent in 1926. The Belgian Chief of the General Staff during the early 1920s, Général Maglinse, supported the French doctrine of strong fortifications along the border regions while another school of thought within the Belgian High Command and political establishment favoured a mobile defence based on a strategic withdrawal to the Scheldt to conform with their French ally in time of war. Neither faction prevailed and the continuing schism ultimately led to compromise. On 22 January 1926, Général Emile Galet replaced Général Maglinse as Chief of Staff. On 18 October 1926, Général Galet proposed to the Minister of National Defence, M. De Broqueville, that a commission be created to investigate the rebuilding of the Belgian fortification system that had been largely destroyed during World War I. The commission delivered its report on 24 February 1927 with the recommendation that a fortified defensive line be constructed on the eastern border along the Meuse River – the *Position Fortifiée de Liège*.

In the best bureaucratic tradition, the defence minister appointed a new 'Commission for the Study of National Fortification' on 21 March 1927 under Général Borremans, the inspector general of the infantry. Its initial meeting was held on 2 April 1927, and the very first mention of the new defensive structure that was to become Fort Eben Emael appeared in a report on the defence of the Limburg region on 24 January 1928.

> On the other hand, faced with the specific danger menacing the area near Maastricht where the Meuse leaves Belgian territory for eight kilometres of its length and where the enclave grows to a width of four kilometres west of the river and faced with the considerable extension of the lines of communication between Aix-la-Chapelle [Aachen] and Maastricht, the Commission has unanimously decided that ... all the main transportation roads and railways converging near Maastricht, the roads leading out of the city and the enclave must be kept within the line of fire of permanent defensive artillery, capable of opening fire within seconds to avoid a surprise attack via Zuid Limburg and all its consequences for the Liège defences.
>
> The Commission has also agreed that these permanent armed defensive structures (estimated to contain a battery of four guns of 150 or 105mm) must be part of a larger line to be erected on the flanks of the Loen and that this group of structures should be supported by a permanent garrison ...

The report calling for the construction of this new fort, as well as the refurbishment of the forts around Liège and Namur, was accepted in principle on 7 January 1929. On 14 May 1929, instructions were issued for the modernization of the six Liège forts on the eastern bank of the Meuse River. These were rearming with modern artillery weapons as well as the refurbished German guns of World War I vintage; improved ventilation systems; and

The creation of the Caster cutting through Mount St Peter was a triumph of civil engineering. It was designed and built by the Belgian company Entreprises Réunies with other companies acting as sub-contractors. These included the German firms of Hochtief A.G. of Essen and Dyckerhoff und Widman of Wiesbaden, but they were not involved with the construction of Fort Eben Emael. There have been several later assertions that these companies had complete plans of the fortress that allowed such a small force as Sturmgruppe Granit to capture Fort Eben Emael so quickly, but that was not the case. This view shows the southern end of the Caster cutting under construction, with the sheer face that formed part of Fort Eben Emael on the left. (Photo Centre de Documentation historiques des Forces armées)

RIGHT The diagram shows the location of the various forts of the *Position Fortifiée de Liège* at the outbreak of World War II. The circles around the various major fortresses represent the ranges of their respective artillery weapons, with the 120mm guns of Fort Eben Emael reaching almost to the German border. The inner circle indicates the range of the 75mm guns, while the innermost one is of the 81mm mortars. The map also shows the various towns, villages and geographical features in the vicinity of Fort Eben Emael that are mentioned in the text, together with the major Belgian army formations in the area. (© Osprey Publishing Ltd)

enhanced protection for the ammunition magazines, as were seven of the nine forts around Namur. Interestingly, the first actual document naming Fort Eben Emael appears in a secret report dated 12 June 1929 of the Deuxième Bureau [French military intelligence] filed by Général Chardigny, the military attaché at the French embassy in Brussels, in which he revealed plans for a fort to be constructed to the north of Liège, in the area of Visé. Indeed as stated previously, it was to be just north of the invasion route of General von Gluck's First Army in 1914, and close to where Général Brialmont had suggested the construction of a fort in 1887: the aphorism of horses and stable doors springs to mind. In a subsequent report to the Ministry of War in Paris on 5 November 1929, Général Chardigny provided specific details of Fort Eben Emael as to its exact location and proposed armament.

The new forts

On 30 June 1930, the occupation of the Rhineland ended and, although now supposedly demilitarized, it no longer provided any buffer zone for the Franco-Belgian alliance from a resurgent Germany. The state of Belgium's defences became evermore critical. As if the dichotomy in the high command was not enough, Belgian domestic internal politics also had a significant influence on defence expenditure and allocation. The country was divided between two distinct ethnic groups that spoke either French in Wallonia, the southern part, or Flemish in the northern part. It was, and remains, a seriously divisive issue. On 10 December 1930, the findings of the 'Commission for the Study of National Fortification' were presented to the cabinet and subsequently to parliament on 11/12 March 1931. They proposed the continued modernization of the forts around Liège together with those of Namur and Antwerp, as well as the construction of a new fort near the village of Eben Emael and defence works around Ghent.

None of the various factions was overly happy with the plan and intense political lobbying ensued with the Walloons being particularly incensed that their region close to Luxembourg remained virtually undefended. Their cause was embraced by the liberal politician Albert Devèze (formerly and subsequently Minister of National Defence). It provoked a political crisis that engulfed King Albert I. Compromises were sought but eventually the Superior Council for National Defence under the direction of King Albert promulgated its decision on 21 April 1931. It endorsed the modernization and extension of the PFL with several new forts including Eben Emael; the abandonment of new fortifications for Antwerp and Ghent; and the creation of a new army formation, the Chasseurs Ardennais, tasked with the defence of the Ardennes region. The modernized forts around Liège were known as *Position Fortifiée de Liège* 2 or PFL 2 and the new forts, *Position Fortifiée de Liège* 1 as they were closer to the border with Germany.

In the following year Albert Devèze became the Minister of National Defence once more. He was determined to implement the plan for strong fortifications along Belgium's eastern border and his promise to the Walloons to defend their interests. The debate as to the allocation of defence funds was rekindled. The Minister of National Defence was adamant that any invasion from the east must be contained at the border. When his Chief of the General Staff, General Galet, disagreed he was forced to retire on 26 December 1932 to be replaced by General Nuyten. In the meantime, military engineers conducted field reconnaissance trips to determine the best locations for the defensive fortifications. On the Herve Plateau, Battice and Tancrémont were chosen as sites for two new powerful forts that greatly enhanced the defences of Liège and Visé. Meanwhile, on 1 April 1932, the first construction works began on the site for the fort of Eben Emael.

On 25 June 1932, an appropriation of 50 million Belgian Francs was sought from the 1933 defence budget for the initial construction of new forts at Battice

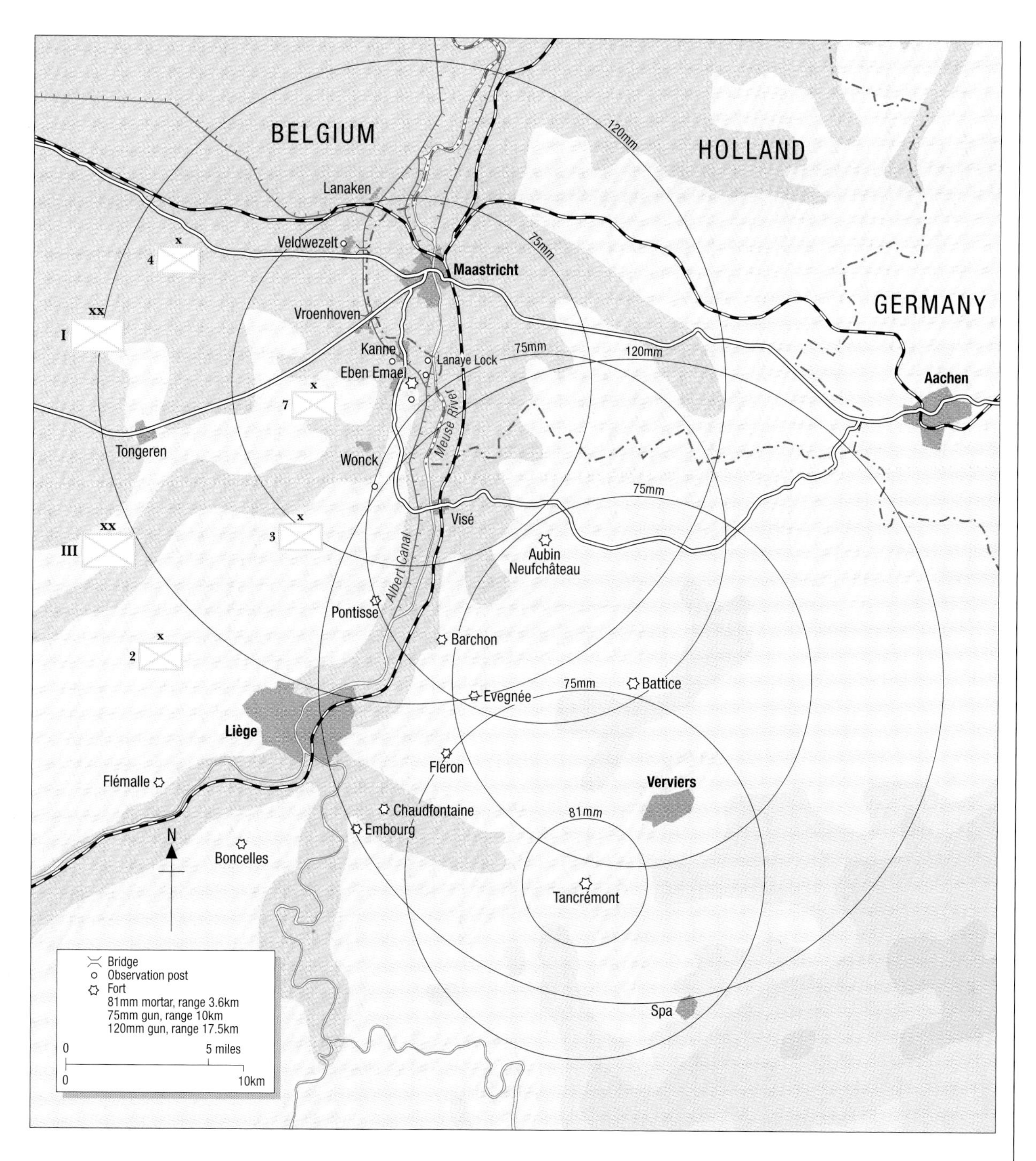

and Tancrémont. However, on 18 August 1932, a budgetary crisis effectively denied this request and on 7 September it was decided to postpone further expenditure on the new defence line, although the purchase of the land at Battice was undertaken. Nevertheless, the 'Commission for the Study of National Fortification' continued its deliberations. Besides the two large forts at Battice and Tancrémont, it recommended a further two smaller ones near Mauhin and Les Waides for the defence of the Herve Plateau. In addition, there were to be numerous infantry bunkers and machine-gun pillboxes to supplement the major forts.

The delays in the construction of the new forts and the defences of the eastern border were now a cause of serious concern, compounded by a failure

Named after King Albert I (1875–1934), the extension of the Albert Canal to avoid the waterway passing through Dutch territory was inaugurated on 30 May 1930 after a prodigious engineering endeavour to cut through Mount St Peter and create the Caster cutting. With the Lanaye locks to the right linking the original Albert Canal with the Meuse River, the cutting created a natural defensive position that became Fort Eben Emael, close to the site recommended by Général Henri Brialmont as long ago as 1890, to form the northern fortress of the *Position Fortifiée de Liège*.

of communications between the various army departments tasked with the enterprise. To remedy the situation, the 'Technical Committee for Fortifications' was formed on 9 January 1933 with the backing of the Minister of National Defence, Albert Devèze. The latter also forced a bill through parliament to expedite the appropriation of funds. Throughout the year construction work at Fort Eben Emael continued apace. Following a council of ministers presided over by the King on 11 October 1933, definitive plans emerged for the defence of the realm. The construction of the forts of Battice and Tancrémont was the priority, together with another major fort at Aubin-Neufchateau in place of those at Mauhin and Les Waides. This allowed greater coverage of the major road running between Aachen in Germany and Visé.

These forts were built between 1935 and 1940 and featured weapon systems similar to those of Fort Eben Emael, although their armoured protection was greater as they were closer to the German border. In all, the cost of construction of these forts together with Fort Eben Emael was in the region of 250 million Belgian Francs. Nevertheless, there still remained a vociferous faction within the army that believed the money would be better spent on a radical reorganization of the army and the mechanization of the cavalry with modern armoured fighting vehicles. Defence procurement has always been dependent on many, often conflicting, factors that must assess potential threats and seek countermeasures to them. The Belgian forts were a prime example of facing the realities of a previous war, yet the actual threat of another invasion from the east seemed genuine and the prime responsibility of any government is to ensure the security of its people. The construction of the most powerful fortresses in the world seemed to fulfil that obligation.

Chronology

21 July 1831 Belgium declares independence from the Netherlands.

19 April 1839 Major European powers guarantee Belgian neutrality with the Treaty of London.

1870–1871 Franco-Prussian War prompts Belgium to build new fortifications around its key cities of Antwerp, Liège and Namur.

1890 Completion of the Brialmont forts of the *Position Fortifiée de Liège* and *Position Fortifiée de Namur* protecting Belgium from invasion from Germany and France respectively.

3 August 1914 Germany declares war on France and invades Belgium.

4 August 1914 Britain and Belgium declare war after German troops enter Belgium. The Liège forts resist until 18 August while those of Namur fall after only four days to heavy German artillery.

1932–1935 Construction of Fort Eben Emael guarding the junction of the Meuse River and the Albert Canal north of Liège.

7 March 1937 German troops march into the demilitarized zone of the Rhineland in contravention of the Versailles Treaty.

1939
1 September Germany invades Poland
3 September France and Great Britain declare war on Germany

1940
10 May Fall Gelb – the German offensive in the west begins.
0400hrs – German gliders are sighted over Belgian territory. The Belgian government appeals to Great Britain and France for assistance.
0430hrs – German Army Group B under General von Bock advances towards the Belgian defensive line along the Albert Canal. German Army Group A under General von Rundstedt strikes through the Ardennes between Liège and the Moselle.
0424hrs – The first of nine gliders carrying Sturmgruppe Granit assault pioneers lands atop Fort Eben Emael. The assault pioneers use novel shaped charges to silence the guns of Europe's most powerful fortress in just 30 minutes. German troops seize intact two out of three bridges across the Albert Canal.
0630hrs – General Gamelin orders Allied troops into Belgium.
11 May 1215hrs Fort Eben Emael surrenders.
20 May Forty allied divisions are trapped in Flanders.
21 May Fort Aubin-Neufchateau surrenders.
22 May Fort Battice surrenders.
28 May At 0400hrs, King Leopold III surrenders to the Germans.
29 May Fort Tancrémont surrenders.

F
G
K
5
E
7
4
D
C
3
S
B
2
U
A
R
T

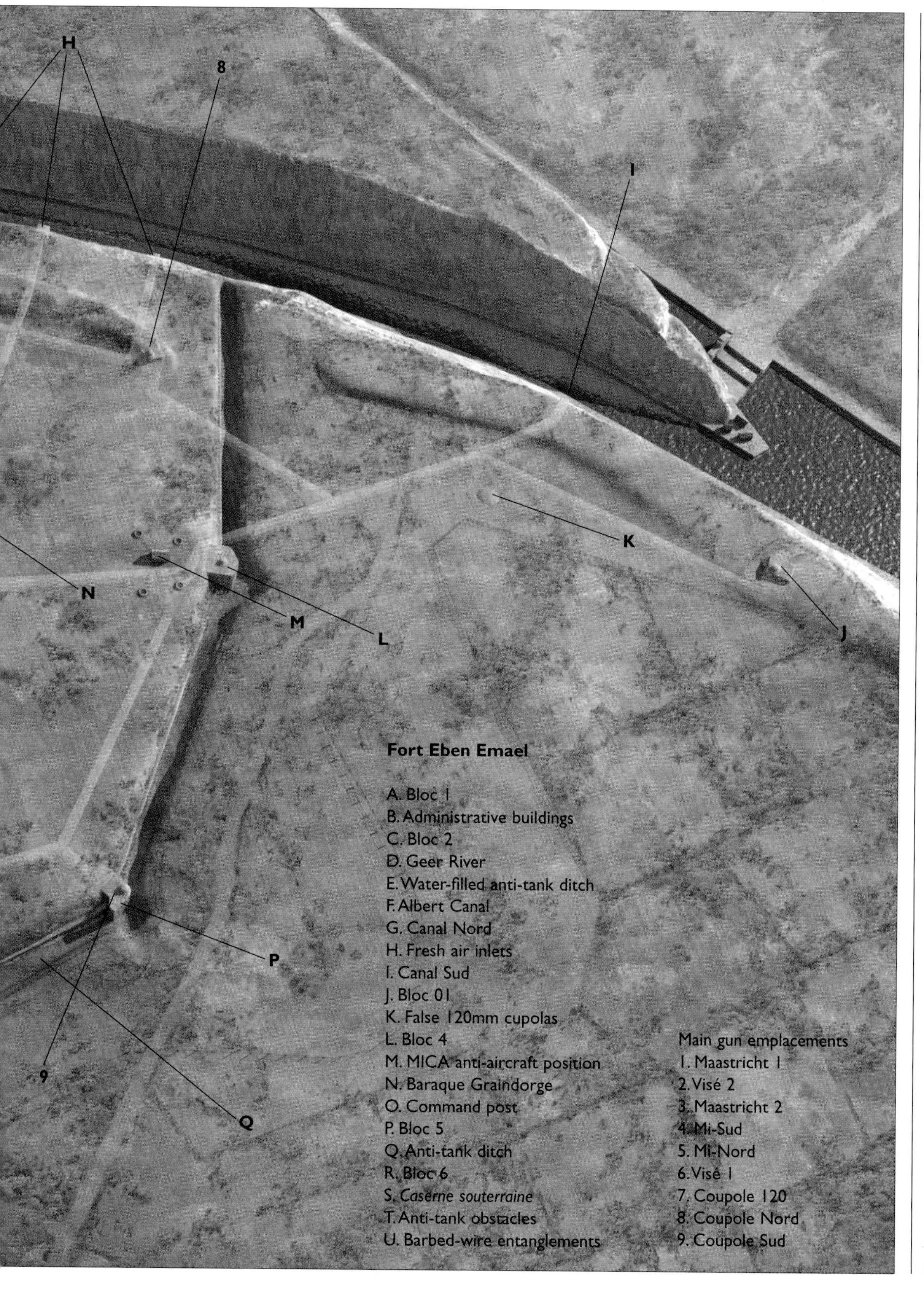
H
8
I
K
N
M
L
J
P
9
Q
Fort Eben Emael
A. Bloc 1
B. Administrative buildings
C. Bloc 2
D. Geer River
E. Water-filled anti-tank ditch
F. Albert Canal
G. Canal Nord
H. Fresh air inlets
I. Canal Sud
J. Bloc 01
K. False 120mm cupolas
L. Bloc 4
M. MICA anti-aircraft position
N. Baraque Graindorge
O. Command post
P. Bloc 5
Q. Anti-tank ditch
R. Bloc 6
S. *Caserne souterraine*
T. Anti-tank obstacles
U. Barbed-wire entanglements
Main gun emplacements
1. Maastricht 1
2. Visé 2
3. Maastricht 2
4. Mi-Sud
5. Mi-Nord
6. Visé 1
7. Coupole 120
8. Coupole Nord
9. Coupole Sud

Fort Eben Emael

The German invasion of Belgium at the outbreak of World War I confirmed Général Brialmont's earlier assessment in 1887 that a fort was necessary to protect the town of Visé through which General von Gluck's powerful First Army swept in August 1914. However, of equal importance was a fort to dominate the bridges connecting Belgium and Holland over the newly created Albert Canal. This was inaugurated on 30 May 1930, connecting Antwerp with Liège by a modern, uninterrupted waterway within Belgium's national boundaries. The actual site for the new fort was determined by the course of the Albert Canal itself. This began at the Lanaye locks on the Meuse River and ran through a channel carved out of a massive hill feature known as Mount St Peter that was some 40m high and dominated the surrounding terrain as far as the German border. Known as the Caster cutting and some 1,300m long, it was a remarkable engineering feat by the standards of the day and its high sheer sides created a natural defensive position on the heights.

Planning for the fort continued through 1931 and construction began on 1 April 1932, under the supervision of Commandant Jean Mercier of the Corps of Engineers. Major works were completed in 1935 when the fort was declared operational, although modifications and improvements continued until May 1940. The fortress was shaped like a diamond with the narrowest point at its northern tip some 40m above the surrounding terrain and directed towards the city of Maastricht. From north to south it was some 900m long and 700m wide with an area of approximately 66 hectares (the equivalent of 70 American football pitches) of which some 40 were fairly level ground. It was here that the fort's main weapon systems were situated. To the north-east, the fortress was protected by the sheer face of the Caster cutting. To the west lay the Geer River, which allowed the approaches from that direction to be flooded. In addition, a 450m-long, 10m-wide concrete-lined anti-tank ditch was dug along the side of the fort that ran southwards from the Albert Canal. This anti-tank ditch was rendered a greater obstacle to tanks and infantry by being filled with water fed

The configuration of the anti-tank ditch with its deep sides and concrete walls is readily apparent from this view looking towards Bloc 4 from Bloc 5. At the left of the photograph, on the skyline, is the armoured dome of Coupole Nord. Out of picture to the immediate left was the MICA anti-aircraft machine-gun position. It is apparent how little cover there was from the Belgian guns in the various casemates on the perimeter of Fort Eben Emael, and one of the reasons why it was thought to be impregnable to conventional attack.

Along the western edge of the fortress was a 450m-long water-filled anti-tank ditch facing northwards towards the Albert Canal while to the left was the Geer River, which fed water into the anti-tank ditch. The right-hand photograph shows a view of the anti-tank ditch from the bank of the Albert Canal looking southwards towards Bloc 2, with the fortress up the hillside on the left. It was along this pathway that Hauptfeldwebel Portsteffen and I Zug of Pionierbataillon 51 made their way to affect the belated link-up with Sturmgruppe Granit. Hauptfeldwebel Portsteffen and I Zug subsequently mounted an attack on Bloc 2 with flamethrowers and explosives to consolidate the situation. Portsteffen took many of the black and white photographs featured in this book soon after the assault. For his gallantry and outstanding leadership during the battle for Fort Eben Emael, Hauptfeldwebel Portsteffen was awarded the Ritterkreuz. The original plans for Fort Eben Emael incorporated a Bloc 3 at the northern tip of the fortress, but subterranean geological faults in the limestone precluded its completion, although a gallery was started from Mi-Nord. Thereafter, a cupola armed with an 81mm mortar and machine guns was envisaged, but it was never built and two false 120mm cupolas were installed instead.

from the Geer River. A 10m-wide, 4m-deep concrete anti-tank ditch with extensive barbed-wire entanglements and steel anti-tank obstacles bordered the southern flanks of the fortress and covered all approaches. Needless to say, all these defences were covered by fire from various blockhouses located around the perimeter of the fortress at ground level.

The blockhouses

At the south-western point of the fortress was Bloc 1. This two-storey structure was the only entrance into the heart of the fortress. It was armed with two 60mm anti-tank guns and three machine guns, as well as two searchlights. The entrance itself featured a heavy gate, and the roadway into the fortress incorporated a retractable wooden section that created a 4m-deep gap impassable to men and vehicles. This in turn was protected by a further machine-gun emplacement in a protective embrasure to engage any enemy that penetrated the outer defences. Anyone who tried to scale the gap in the roadway could also be eliminated by grenades dropped through special slots in the wall. The fields of fire of the weapons of Bloc 1 interlocked with those of Blocs 2 and 6 to cover the approaches from the south and west. On top of Bloc 1 was an armoured observation dome covering the surrounding terrain. The manpower for Bloc 1 comprised five NCOs and 23 soldiers.

Bloc 2 was located some 200m north of Bloc 1, and was situated at the head of the water-filled anti-tank ditch on the western flank of the fortress. It also was armed with two 60mm anti-tank weapons and three machine guns, as well as two searchlights and an armoured observation dome on top. In addition, it featured a sally port to allow personnel to counter-attack from the position. The fields of fire of Bloc 2 extended from the Albert Canal to the north and Bloc 1 to the south. The gun crew of Bloc 2 numbered four NCOs and 22 soldiers. Although planned, there was no Bloc 3, but two special emplacements were built on the banks of the Albert Canal covering the approaches along the waterway and its towpaths. These were two-storey structures built into the sheer wall of the Caster cutting. They were known as Canal Nord and Canal Sud and, being some 800m apart, they were mutually supporting. Canal Nord was armed with a 60mm anti-tank gun, one machine gun and a searchlight covering the Albert Canal towards the village and bridge at Kanne, and two machine guns pointing in the other direction towards the Lanaye locks and Canal Sud. The latter had the same weapons but with the converse arrangement of its 60mm anti-tank gun covering the Lanaye locks and Meuse River. Both emplacements featured an armoured observation dome on top incorporating firing ports for an FM 30 machine gun and a flare gun, either for signalling or illuminating the canal. These domes were considerably larger than

RIGHT Bloc 1 was the main entrance to Fort Eben Emael. It was located at the south-western point of the fortress and faced the village after which the fort was named. This photograph was taken on the approach road to Bloc 1, soon after the capture of Fort Eben Emael. Above Bloc 1 on the skyline is the dome of the main air ventilation outlet. Trupp 3 attacked this structure after they had disabled their primary target of Maastricht 1. At 0445hrs, a 3kg charge was dropped down the ventilation shaft causing consternation amongst the underground garrison. Fortunately for them, Trupp 3 did not continue the attack as further explosives could have seriously damaged the ventilation system. Indeed, a new ventilation system had recently been installed for the fort, but it proved inadequate during the course of the battle and the garrison had to revert to the old one.

LEFT Bloc 2 was located on the western side of the fortress at the head of the water-filled anti-tank ditch that ran to the Albert Canal. Its guns dominated the ground to the north and they also interlocked with those of Bloc 1 to the south. Stuka dive-bombers attacked Bloc 2 soon after the assault began. At 0630hrs, Trupp 3 detonated a 50kg hollow-charge weapon above the armoured observation dome killing the soldier inside. Several Belgian counter-attacks were mounted up the hillside to the right of Bloc 2 as shown here. Those undertaken by the soldiers of the garrison at 0600hrs and 0800hrs were ineffective as they had no infantry training or modern weapons. Further counter-attacks over this ground were mounted by men of the 1er Companie of the 2e Grenadiers around midday. Sporadic fighting continued around Maastricht 1 until 1700hrs, during which Oberjäger Hübel and Gefreiter Jürgensen of Trupp 10, and Gefreiter Kruck of Trupp 11, were killed. Feldwebel Wenzel was also injured when a bullet grazed his head around 1500hrs. It was at Bloc 2 that the first contact between the men of Pionierbataillon 51 and Sturmgruppe Granit occurred, but not until 0500hrs on 11 May 1940, some 18 hours behind schedule.

A view of the Albert Canal as it passes through the Caster cutting with Mount St Peter to the left and the sheer wall of the north-eastern side of Fort Eben Emael to the right. With a height of 40m it presented a formidable obstacle to any attacker. Built into the side of the fortress, along the western bank of the canal, were two defence works, Canal Nord and Canal Sud. These were armed with 60mm anti-tank guns, machine guns, and searchlights that dominated all approaches along the canal. During the battle, fire from Canal Sud destroyed a German machine-gun post at Lanaye, and fire from Canal Nord caused serious delays to the men of Pionierbataillon 51 trying to cross the canal in order to relieve the exhausted paratroopers of Sturmgruppe Granit. Realizing the threat posed by Canal Nord, the men of Trupp 6 under the command of Oberjäger Harlos made several attempts during the night to destroy the position by lowering demolition charges on long lengths of rope, but with only limited success. Dirt from the explosions managed to obscure the optics of the armoured observation dome, but the 60mm anti-tank gun continued to fire on German positions in Kanne and around the destroyed bridge. It finally fell silent after a technical fault.

those on top of the fort. There were also emergency exits and hand grenade slots. Each gun emplacement had 36 Mills No. 36 hand grenades for this purpose. The crew of each position numbered three NCOs and 17 soldiers.

Bloc 4 was located on the south-eastern side of the fortress with fields of fire extending from the Albert Canal to Bloc 5 and Coupole Sud. It covered all approaches along the anti-tank ditch. It was armed with two 60mm anti-tank guns, two machine guns, as well as two searchlights, and had an armoured observation dome on top. It had a crew of four NCOs and 22 soldiers. Bloc 5 was situated on the south-eastern tip of the diamond-shaped fortress. It was unusual in that it provided covering fire over the anti-tank ditch and featured one of the retractable armoured gun emplacements, Coupole Sud, on top, of which more later. Bloc 5 was armed with one 60mm anti-tank gun and two machine guns, as well as a searchlight, and had an armoured observation dome. It could only fire in one direction, towards Bloc 6. Its crew numbered three NCOs and 14 soldiers.

Bloc 4 was typical of the casemates protecting the southern and eastern sides of the fortress. Together with Blocs 5 and 6, these gun emplacements dominated the anti-tank ditches, and covered with fire the anti-tank obstacles and barbed wire entanglements to the south and east. Readily visible is the armoured observation dome that was destroyed by a 50kg charge detonated by Trupp 5 under the command of Feldwebel Haug. In the background to the right on the skyline is the dome of the third false cupola of Fort Eben Emael that was located outside the actual perimeter of the fortress and near to Bloc 01. The sheet steel dome is now on display outside Bloc 1 at the entrance to Fort Eben Emael as a museum exhibit.

Bloc 6 completed the ring of gun emplacements circling the fortress, and it could also only fire in one direction, towards Bloc 1. It was armed with two 60mm anti-tank guns, two machine guns, and a searchlight. It also had an armoured observation dome. The latter weighed 6,700kg with a height of 150cm and an interior diameter of 80cm, which gave only sufficient room for a single observer. The armour thickness was 20cm, and each dome incorporated four observation slits of armoured glass that could be covered with metal shutters. The dome was designed to be proof against artillery bursts of up to 22cm calibre. The searchlights were of two types and were housed in a revolving armoured cylinder. The Willocq-Bottin model had an effective range of 225m and the GZ33 type a range of 700m. Bloc 6 had a crew of three NCOs and 17 soldiers.

The gun emplacements

These perimeter defences were designed to thwart attack from any direction, but the fundamental purpose of the fortress was as an impregnable artillery battery that dominated the surrounding terrain as far as the German border. To this end, a variety of gun emplacements were landscaped into the top superstructure of the fortress. As the three bridges over the Albert Canal carrying the roads and their approaches from the Dutch town of Maastricht were the priority targets for the fort, two casemates, each containing three 75mm quick-firing cannons, were configured in their direction. They were known as Maastricht 1 and Maastricht 2. Maastricht 1 was landscaped into the hilly north-western flank of the fortress, while Maastricht 2 was on top of the superstructure. The latter also incorporated an armoured observation dome on its roof to allow direct vision over the Albert Canal and into the Maastricht enclave. However, by the terms of Belgian neutrality, the guns were not allowed to fire onto Dutch territory. The guns had a field of fire of 70 degrees, with an elevation of –5 to +37 degrees, a range of 11km and a rate of fire of ten rounds

The main triple 75mm gun casemates were named after the towns that their weapons covered with fire. Visé 1 faced southwards, as did Visé 2, and so they were not primary targets for Sturmgruppe Granit as their guns did not threaten the bridges over the Albert Canal. However, Visé 1 was the secondary target for Trupp 2, as its guns did dominate the surface of the fortress and so were a threat to the assault pioneers. As Trupp 2 never arrived at the fortress, the task was given to Trupp 10, and one 75mm gun was destroyed by a 12.5kg charge causing the Belgian gun crew to withdraw to the intermediate level. At 0510hrs, Maj. Jottrand issued a fire mission but as there were no men present this was impossible. Accordingly, Maj. Jottrand informed the headquarters at Liège that Visé 1 was out of action. Sometime later, Lt. Desloovere returned to the gun gallery and further rounds were fired to the south. Any further fire was stopped by the command post at 1030hrs on the pretext that a counter-attack was to be mounted on the top of the fortress. At 1300hrs, the Germans silenced the guns of Visé 1 forever by detonating 1kg charges in their barrels. In the left background of the top photograph is the gun emplacement Mi-Nord. The two casemates were linked by an earth rampart to landscape them into the terrain, and obscure observation of the fortress from the top of Mount St Peter across the Albert Canal. At the time of the assault, all the casemates were painted in earth-coloured stripes of brown and green and were masked with camouflage netting.

The retractable armoured gun emplacement Coupole Sud was not a primary target for Sturmgruppe Granit. As it was located at the southern tip of the fortress, the Germans did not believe that its guns could fire on the bridges over the Albert Canal to the north. Although attacked with a 50kg hollow-charge weapon during the initial assault, Coupole Sud remained in action throughout the battle. Around 0745hrs, it obtained canister rounds from the ammunition magazines of Coupole Nord. With these rounds lashing the top of the fortress, the troops of Sturmgruppe Granit were forced to take cover inside the captured casemates. If these canister rounds had been available prior to the glider landings, the outcome of the attack might have been very different. During the course of the battle, Coupole Sud fired several fire missions under the direction of observers in EBEN 1, located above Bloc 01 overlooking the Lanaye locks and the Albert Canal to the south. From 1030hrs, Coupole Sud laid effective fire on the German 269th Infantry Division in the village of Eysden, and also destroyed a pontoon bridge over the Meuse River. At the time of the surrender, Coupole Sud was put out of action by retracting the armoured dome and firing the 75mm guns underground.

a minute per gun. There were two similar casemates configured to fire to the south towards the town of Visé to cover the bridges across the Meuse River. These casemates were known as Visé 1 and Visé 2. Again, Visé 2 was landscaped into the southern flank of the fortress while Visé 1 was on top. These casemates each had a crew of five NCOs and 28 soldiers, although Maastricht 2 had an additional three personnel who acted as observers for EBEN 3, the armoured observation dome on top of the position.

Each of the casemates had two floors, with the upper gallery containing the three 75mm guns and their crews as well as telephonists to relay the fire direction orders from the fortress command post. The gunners of these casemates had limited direct vision with the outside world and relied on pre-planned fire orders that gave the bearing and elevation to engage the requisite target, be it a bridge or an approach road. On the lower floor were the ammunition store and the lift mechanisms to convey the rounds to the guns. The casemates were built of reinforced concrete up to 2.75m thick, capable of sustaining prolonged bombardment from 22cm artillery rounds and all contemporary aerial bombs. Furthermore, the chances of being struck through the bombing techniques of the day were negligible, and reduced further by the clever landscaping of the casemates, which were painted to conform with the surrounding vegetation and concealed behind permanent camouflage netting to disguise them from aerial observation by reconnaissance aircraft. Throughout the late 1930s civilian Ju52s of Lufthansa, the German national airline, regularly carried aerial cameras to photograph installations of interest to the German High Command across Europe, including Fort Eben Emael.

While these four casemates were configured to bombard the specific targets of the bridges to the north and south of the fortress, there were further gun

Visé 2

The principal weapon systems of Fort Eben Emael were the four triple 75mm gun casemates covering the towns of Maastricht and Visé. None of the other forts in the *Position Fortifiée de Liège* had such gun emplacements. The latter were configured on three levels with the main ammunition magazines on the intermediate level of the fortress separated from the actual gun emplacement by two pairs of armoured double doors. The ammunition rounds were transported from the magazines by handcarts through the armoured doors and by means of lifts to the lower gallery of the gun emplacement. This level contained the ammunition storerooms and preparation areas for the rounds such as cleaning and fusing as well as the latrines for the gun crew that comprised five NCOs and 28 soldiers. The rounds were then passed up to the top level by three lifts two of which were situated in the centre of the stairwell that allowed the crew access to the gunroom. The 75mm quick-firing guns were based on the Krupp 1905 model that had been in service with the Belgian army since before the Great War. The guns had a field of fire in azimuth of 70 degrees with an elevation of –5 to +37 degrees. They had a maximum range of 11km and a rate of fire of ten rounds a minute per gun. Above each gun was a telescopic sight for direct vision of the fortress roof in case of infantry attack but most artillery engagements relied on pre-planned fire orders that gave the bearing and elevation to engage the requisite target be it a bridge or an approach road. This type of fire mission was known as *feu d'interdiction* as it was intended to deny all the approaches of the Albert Canal bridges to the enemy. The fire orders came from the command post and were relayed to the gun crew by two telephonists in the upper level. The 75mm guns fired three types of rounds with two being high explosive and the other canister. The earlier model 75mm HE round had a range of 8km and contained 800g of explosive while the later round had a range of 11km and contained 650g of explosive. Accordingly, these rounds were not heavy enough to cause any serious damage to the bridges themselves; for this reason the bridges were rigged with demolition charges if their destruction was necessary. The third type of round was a canister round that contained 234 12g lead balls for engaging troops in the open. The casemates were built of reinforced concrete up to 2.75m thick capable of sustaining prolonged bombardment from 22cm artillery rounds and all contemporary aerial bombs. The exteriors were painted in green and brown stripes and all the gun emplacements were masked from aerial observation by camouflage netting.

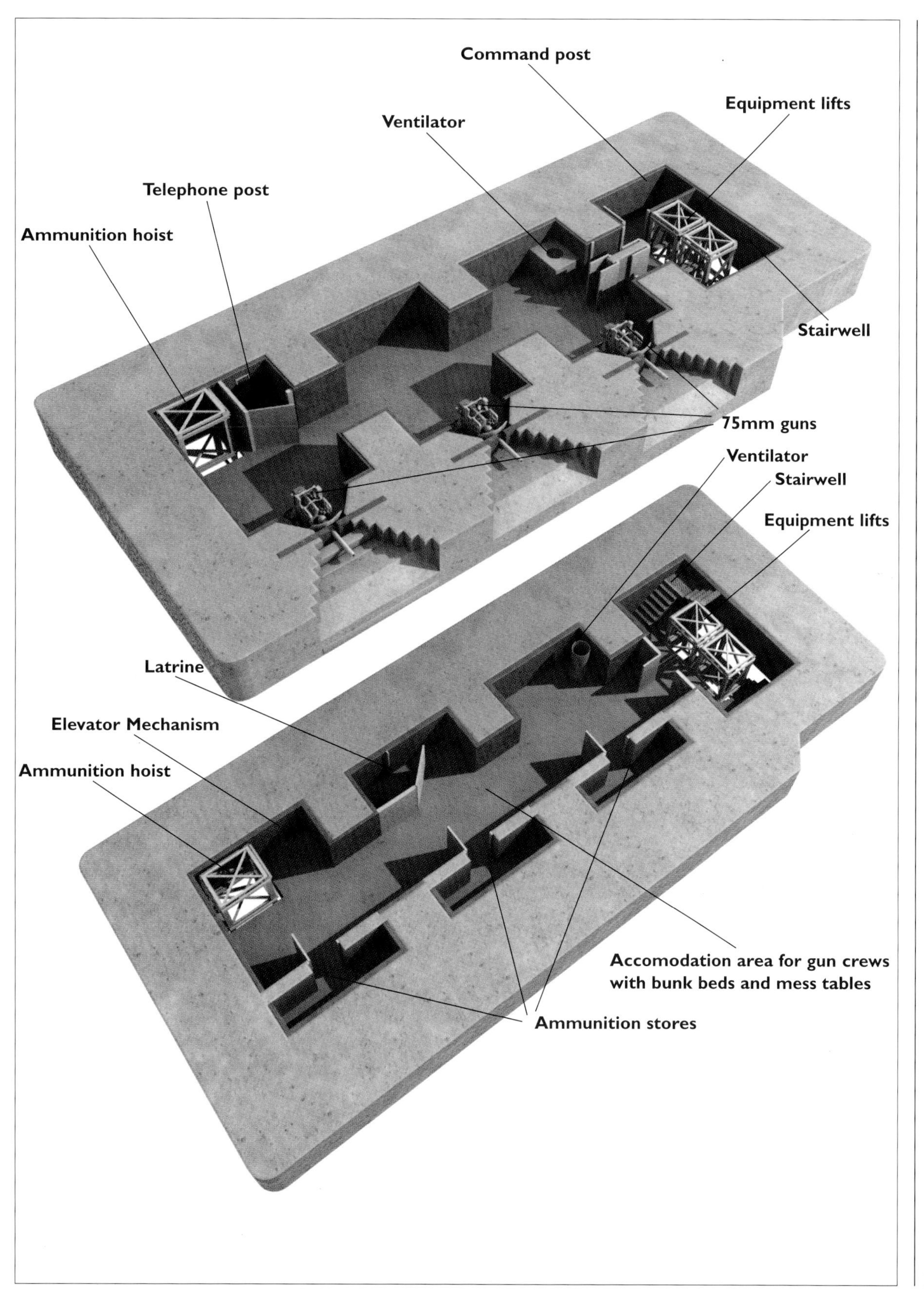
Command post
Equipment lifts
Ventilator
Telephone post
Ammunition hoist
Stairwell
75mm guns
Ventilator
Stairwell
Equipment lifts
Latrine
Elevator Mechanism
Ammunition hoist
Accomodation area for gun crews
with bunk beds and mess tables
Ammunition stores

emplacements to engage targets of opportunity. Two of these were heavily armoured retractable cupolas armed with twin 75mm guns. These were known as Coupole Nord and Coupole Sud due to their geographical location on top of the fortress. Despite its name, Coupole Nord was located on the south-eastern tip of the fortress where the diamond shape is at its broadest. Its twin, Coupole Sud, was installed above Bloc 5 at the southernmost point of the fortress. Both emplacements were capable of 360-degree rotation to allow their 75mm guns to fire in any direction. On a given fire mission, the armoured cupola rose 53cm out of the ground to reveal its twin 75mm guns and the aiming periscope in between. Once the fire mission was complete, the cupola sank into the ground where its armoured carapace made it immune to attack by conventional explosives. The outer shell was a single armoured casting 38cm thick, with two inner layers of steel plates, each 2.5cm thick, interspersed with a felt material lining. This configuration reduced the shock effect on the inside following any explosion on the exterior of the cupola. The interior was also sealed against gas attack. The gun crew comprised three NCOs and 22 soldiers.

The revolving cupola and gunroom weighed 120 tons and was raised by a counterweight, with the power for elevation and rotation provided by electric motors with a manual override in case of malfunction. Five men operated the guns, two loaders per gun and a gunlayer seated between them manning the periscope and receiving fire orders through his headphones. The Modèle 1934 FRC (Fonderies Royales de Canons) 75mm gun was specially designed for this weapon system. With an elevation of –8 to +38 degrees, it had a range of 10km and a maximum rate of fire of 25 rounds a minute, with a sustained rate of half that. The guns fired two types of high explosives and a special canister round. Similar to a giant shotgun cartridge, the latter was designated *Boîte à balles*, and contained 205 lead balls each of 1.5cm diameter for engaging personnel on top of the fortress. With a range of 200m, it was a devastating weapon against troops in the open.

Mi-Nord was a critical target for Sturmgruppe Granit as its machine guns dominated the landing ground of the DFS 230 gliders. Although manned at the outset of the attack, the Belgian defenders were forbidden to open their ammunition boxes, and by the time they saw their attackers it was too late. After destroying the armoured observation dome EBEN 2 on top, the men of Trupp 4, under the command of Feldwebel Wenzel, blasted their way into the casemate with a 50kg charge. The Belgian gun crew withdrew to the intermediate level. Once inside the devastated casemate, Fw. Wenzel groped around in the billowing smoke when suddenly the telephone rang. Wenzel later recalled that it was the one moment of the attack that he was truly frightened. Nevertheless, he picked up the phone to hear someone speaking in a language he could not understand. With no knowledge of French, he replied in English – 'Here are the Germans' to which the response came – 'Oh mon Dieu!' and the telephone was disconnected. Wenzel subsequently destroyed the staircase down to the intermediate level to prevent any counter-attack by the Belgians. Mi-Nord became the German command post and field dressing station throughout the battle.

Mi-Sud was the companion gun emplacement to Mi-Nord. Both were armed with three double machine guns, and had armoured observation domes on top. That of Mi-Sud was capable of being fitted with a light machine gun. Mi-Sud was attacked by Trupp 9 commanded by Oberjäger Neuhaus, with a 50kg lodged into the southward facing machine-gun embrasure. The resulting hole in the structure allowed Trupp 9 entry into the gun emplacement, where they took up a defensive posture. Again, like Mi-Nord, the stairwell was destroyed with explosives to prevent a Belgian counter-attack.

At the level below the gunroom, the ammunition was prepared by 14 soldiers and an NCO and then loaded into hoists that served the guns. The third level comprised a machinery room to power the cupola with an electrician and three other artificers in attendance. The fourth and last level housed the main ammunition magazine, where ten soldiers and an NCO retrieved the types and quantities of rounds required by the gunroom. These were transported by handcarts to the ammunition lifts that conveyed them to the second level. The two cupolas were thus able to engage targets anywhere within a 10km radius and even targets on the fortress itself. Coupole Nord also incorporated an armoured door with an integral machine gun to cover the open spaces atop the fortress and allow a counter-attack in the unlikely event of enemy troops managing to gain the ground. It cannot be said that the designers of Fort Eben Emael did not foresee the need to defend the top of the fortress from infantry attack.

Two additional gun emplacements named Mi-Nord and Mi-Sud reaffirmed this: Mi standing for *mitrailleuse* or machine gun. Their designation reveals their very purpose – the defence of the top of the fortress against enemy infantry. Mi-Nord was located to the north-east of the fortress, with most of its guns dominating the level ground to the south. It was connected to Mi-Sud to the south-west by an earth rampart and barbed wire entanglements. Mi-Nord was also connected by an earth rampart to the Visé 1 casemate to the south-east. These earth ramparts or 'berms' were designed to obscure any direct vision from the top of Mount St Peter, which was slightly higher than Fort Eben Emael. Accordingly, no observer or direct fire weapon on the hill was able to see or fire at any of the gun emplacements on top of the fort. Mi-Nord featured three machine guns and two searchlights, as well as an armoured observation dome known as EBEN 2 that allowed unimpeded vision over the Albert Canal to the north and towards its vital bridges. Like EBEN 1 and 3, this dome incorporated a revolving periscope manufactured by the French firm Société d'Optique Mécanique, which was also used on the Maginot Line. One of Mi-Nord's machine guns pointed northwards towards the Albert Canal, with an additional machine gun protecting the armoured entrance door to the bunker that allowed troops to exit and mount a counter-attack if necessary. Mi-Sud was similarly configured but had an additional searchlight. The interlocking fire of these machine guns, combined with the deadly canister rounds of the 75mm gun emplacements, was more than sufficient to deal with any enemy troops on top of the fortress, even at night when they would be illuminated by the

Coupole 120 was the most powerful gun emplacement of Fort Eben Emael, with a range as far as the German border. As the primary target for Trupp 2, it was spared attack in the initial assault. Unaccountably, its ammunition hoists failed to function, although they worked perfectly the day before. For many years there were dark tales of sabotage, but in all likelihood it was due to the inadequate maintenance procedures of a demoralized garrison. In any event, the guns of Coupole 120 failed to fire a single shot during the battle despite the plethora of targets around Maastricht, let alone the bridges over the Albert Canal. Protruding through the top of the armoured carapace is a periscopic sight; as related in the text, its horizontal telescope was never delivered but it was through this aperture that the gun crew engaged the advancing men of Trupp 5 and their Belgian prisoners with a rifle, wounding at least two. The colour photograph shows Coupole 120 in its dominating position in the centre of the fortress, with Visé I to the right in the background, and the damage caused by a 50kg charge above the left-hand gun.

various searchlights. Beside the three personnel manning EBEN 2, Mi-Nord had a crew of three NCOs and 12 soldiers, while Mi-Sud had a crew of three NCOs and 11 soldiers.

In addition, at the southern end of the fortress was an anti-aircraft gun emplacement comprising four Maxim 7.65mm machine guns (MICA or *Mitrailleuse contre avions*) with each in a separate open gun pit some 25m apart. In the middle of the position was a small hut with a telephone operator who was connected to the command post. The MICA crew comprised one officer, four NCOs and 13 soldiers. Also nearby was a large wooden building known as Baraque Graindorge that acted as a workshop for the armourers form the Foneries Royales de Canons who serviced the guns of the various casemates and cupolas. An additional two machine guns were held in the MICA hut, with another two at the garrison accommodation barracks in the village of Wonck. Many of the machine guns defending the fortress were versions of the Maxim 08 and 08/15 that were the spoils of war from Germany. MAE (Manufacture d'Armes de l'Etat) modified these to fire the Belgian 7.65mm round. A special reversible mounting incorporating two machine guns, one over the other, was designed for installation in forts. This allowed sustained firing, with one gun being reloaded with a 250-round ammunition belt as the other continued firing. The empty cartridge cases were ejected down a tube into a container filled with a caustic soda solution to reduce the build-up of toxic fumes from the spent rounds. All these aspects are indicative of the attention to detail by the designers for the defence of Fort Eben Emael.

But that was not all. Located centrally atop the fortress was its heaviest armament of a massive armoured cupola mounting twin FRC Modèle 31 120mm guns. Unlike Coupoles Nord and Sud, it was not retractable but instead featured two embrasures in the massive casting for the two 120mm guns. This gave rise to its name of Coupole 120. The armoured cupola was 5.75m in diameter and weighed 230 tons. It was anchored in a huge reinforced concrete pit with an additional 210 tons of armour plate protecting the actual gunroom.

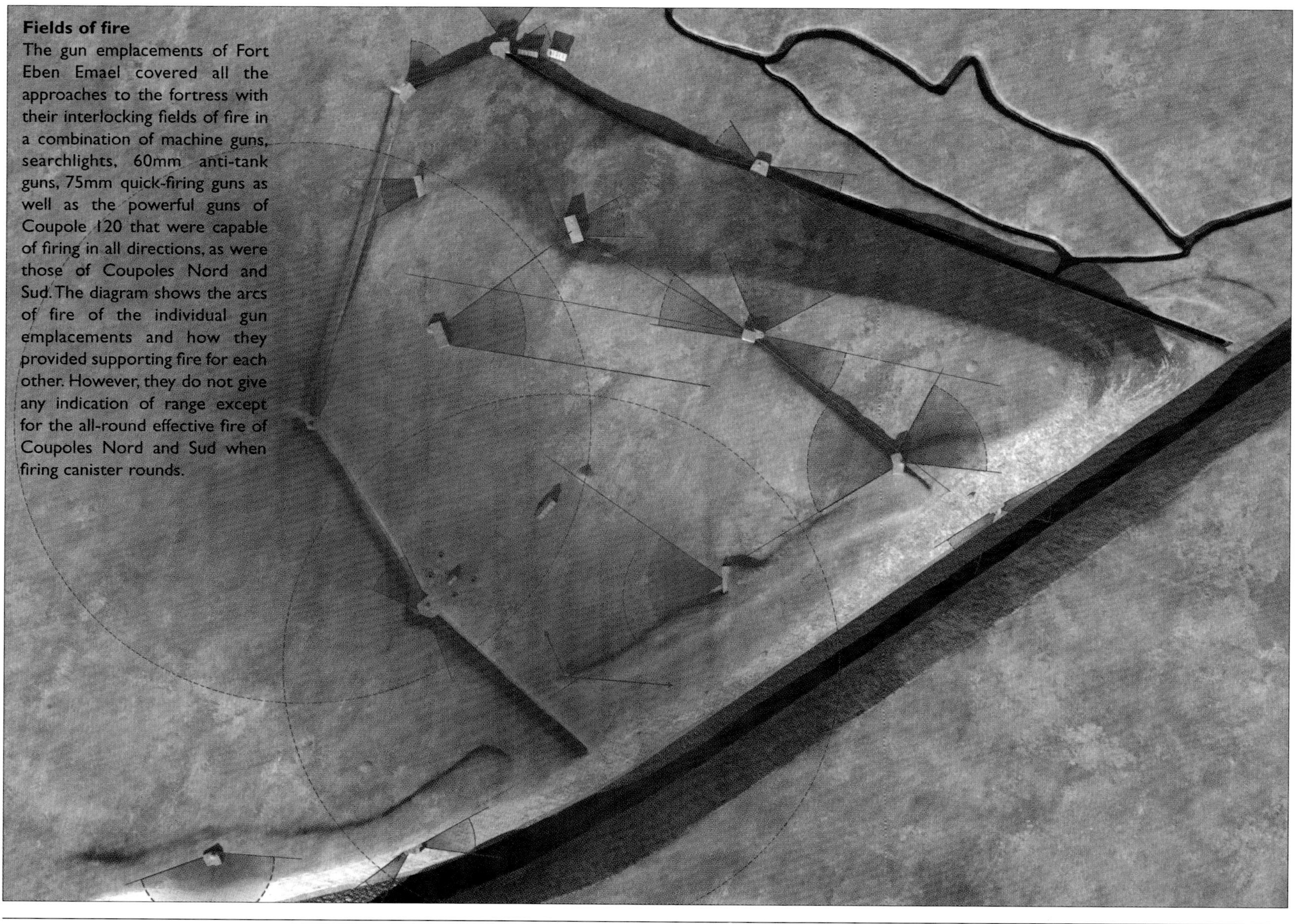

Fields of fire

The gun emplacements of Fort Eben Emael covered all the approaches to the fortress with their interlocking fields of fire in a combination of machine guns, searchlights, 60mm anti-tank guns, 75mm quick-firing guns as well as the powerful guns of Coupole 120 that were capable of firing in all directions, as were those of Coupoles Nord and Sud. The diagram shows the arcs of fire of the individual gun emplacements and how they provided supporting fire for each other. However, they do not give any indication of range except for the all-round effective fire of Coupoles Nord and Sud when firing canister rounds.

Coupole 120 rotated through 360 degrees on 36 conical rollers to allow firing in any direction. The armoured dome comprised a 21cm-thick outer steel alloy shell attached to a 4cm iron shell, followed by a 5cm thick layer of felt padding and another 4cm iron shell, to which was attached the 25cm-thick inner steel alloy shell giving an overall thickness of 59cm. The cupola was on three different levels, with the gunroom at the top and the guns dividing it down the middle. The commander was located on the right-hand side, from where he could observe through the cupola periscope. With him was a gun layer who operated the elevation controls and maintained the right-hand gun. On the other side was another gun layer, who laid the guns in azimuth and maintained the left-hand gun together with a telephonist relaying the fire mission from the command post. On the middle level were the hydraulic pumps and rams to power the heavy cupola and its weapons, as well as 11 soldiers to pack the separated ammunition and set the fuses. On the bottom level was an NCO and another four soldiers, who collected the various projectiles and charges from the ammunition magazine and passed them upwards by hoists. Coupole 120 had a crew of four NCOs and 24 soldiers.

The separated ammunition comprised the projectile and a shell case containing the propellant. The range to target was thus a combination of the elevation of the gun and the amount of propellant packed into the shell case. Two types of high-explosive projectiles were used. The first was a 22kg round containing contact fusing of various delays depending on whether detonation was required on the surface of a target or after penetration. The explosive content was 2.875kg and was colour coded in yellow. The second type of projectile was blue in colour and weighed 20kg. It contained 2kg of explosives and was designed as an airburst weapon against troops in the open. The shell case had a maximum weight of 13kg and held up to five charge bags of nitrocellulose propellant. Coupole 120 had a maximum range of 17.5km and was thus able to engage targets as far as the German border, as well as giving mutual supporting fire to several of the forts in the PFL to the south. It was obviously capable of supplementing the volume of fire of the fixed casemates in their primary mission of destroying the three bridges of the Albert Canal. However, one of its principal roles was to provide counter-battery fire against the kind of siege artillery that had been the cause of the demise of the Liège forts in 1914. As siege artillery howitzers are relatively short-range weapons that rely on high-angle plunging fire for their devastating effect they would become vulnerable to the long reach of Coupole 120. However, these powerful weapons required periodic cooling during sustained fire missions, and there was no provision for water-cooling. Accordingly, the rate of fire was notionally restricted to no more than two rounds per minute for the first five minutes and one round every 40 seconds for the next 15 minutes. To confuse hostile aerial reconnaissance, three dummy cupolas similar in dimensions to Coupole 120 were located atop the fortress with two at the north-west and one to the east near the observation post EBEN 1 overlooking the Albert Canal and the Lanaye locks. These were simply sheet steel domes on a concrete base, but from the air they were indistinguishable from Coupole 120.

Armoured doors

Another lesson drawn from the experiences of World War I and the fate of the Brialmont forts was that instead of grouping all the major weapons and ammunition magazines in close proximity, all the casemates and cupolas of Fort Eben Emael were well dispersed, with most being at least 150m apart and their ammunition magazines buried deep in the bowels of the fortress itself. In the unlikely event that an individual casemate was destroyed or invested by ground attack, its crew could withdraw to a lower level and seal off the fallen position entirely from the interior of the fortress. This was achieved by a system of heavily armoured doors. These came in two pairs that were 2m apart, with both sets of doors closing inwards on themselves. Between the two pairs of doors were slots to accommodate a series of 20cm steel girders that then formed another complete barrier behind the pair of doors closest to the casemate. The gap between the steel girder barrier and the second pair of doors was then filled with sandbags. Finally, the inside doors were closed and locked, creating an obstacle that was virtually immune to conventional explosives, thus denying an enemy any access to the interior of the fortress if a casemate should actually fall. Ordinarily, one set of doors was free of girders and sandbags to allow access for the gun crew to the casemate and the free passage of ammunition. The magazines were located below each gun emplacement. There were 2,000 120mm rounds, 19,200 75mm rounds and 6,000 60mm rounds available for the various guns.

As an integral design feature of Fort Eben Emael, each and every gun emplacement could be isolated from the interior of the fortress by a pair of double armoured doors. Once the outer doors adjacent to the gun emplacement were closed, 8in. steel beams were slotted in behind them as further reinforcement. The 2m gap between the two sets of armoured doors was then filled with sandbags to absorb the force of any conventional explosives. These heavily armoured doors were formidable barriers to thwart any attacker that managed to capture a gun emplacement from entering the fortress.

Caserne Souterraine

The defences of Bloc 1 have been recounted above, but once past the removable wooden roadway there were decontamination rooms to the right for troops who may have been exposed to gas attack. Next there was the machine-gun embrasure and armoured door that barred entry to the fortress itself. This comprised a gallery some 200m long with various workshops, fuel stores, the penitentiary, and separate latrines for officers and other ranks. There then came a slight bend to the left with the electrical powerplant immediately on the right. This comprised six diesel-powered generators of 140 KVA each, of which any two was sufficient to provide the power needs of the fortress at any one time. The cooling water from the generators was used for the central heating system and to heat the showers for the troops. Their washrooms were located nearby and beyond them were the kitchen, canteen and associated storerooms, as well as the fortress commander's administrative offices and the barber's shop. There was sufficient fuel and food to last the garrison for two months.

An intersection divided the gallery with the hospital, operating theatre, and dental surgery to the left and access to the main staircase and elevators to the intermediate level on the right, as well as the extensive accommodation facilities for the officers and other ranks. Access to the intermediate level was through hermetically sealed armoured doors and via a 116-step staircase with an elevation of 21m. The elevators to the intermediate stage were only used for officers and ammunition. The other ranks were obliged to use the staircase and walk everywhere throughout the fortress, whereas the officers were allowed to use bicycles to venture from point to point. The intermediate level comprised all the interconnecting galleries and tunnels to the various gun emplacements and casemates of the fortress, with a total length of some 4km underground. At various intersections, there were machine-gun posts in armoured embrasures to dominate all avenues, making any enemy infiltration a suicidal mission. Also on the intermediate level were the main inlets for the fort's air ventilation system. These were situated on the sheer wall of the Caster cutting overlooking the Albert Canal. The air was vented through a series of filters as protection against poisonous gas. The purified air was then fed into the fortress at atmospheric overpressure to further inhibit the ingress of noxious gases and preclude the garrison from having to wear gas masks during combat action. The major exhaust outlet for the ventilation system and power plant was located above and behind Bloc 1, equidistant between casemates Maastricht 1 and Visé 2. Also on the intermediate level was the *poste de commandement*, or command post, from where all the gun emplacements on the top level were issued fire missions based on information from various observation posts on top of the fortress and in the surrounding countryside, as well as other army units in the region.

Observation posts

The most important of these on the fortress was Bloc 01 although it was situated just outside the main complex overlooking the Albert Canal, Meuse River and Lanaye locks with a view all the way to the German border. Its armoured observation dome was designated EBEN 1. From its dominating position, Bloc 01 was able to observe all movement over a wide area as far south as Visé and thus provide fire missions for Visé 1 and Visé 2 as well as Coupoles 120, Nord and Sud as necessary. Beside EBEN 1, it featured one 60mm anti-tank gun, three machine guns, and three searchlights. Bloc 01 had a crew of four NCOs and 18 soldiers, as well as three observers for EBEN 1. EBEN 2 on top of Mi-Nord had a field of view northwards over the Albert Canal towards the village of Kanne, as did EBEN 3 on top of Maastricht 2, although being at a lower elevation its field of view was not so extensive northwards. It did, however, have unimpeded direct vision over much of the top of the fortress and thus was able to coordinate the response to any infantry attack in the vicinity. These armoured observation domes formed the eyes of Fort Eben Emael and were vital for its proper functioning as an artillery battery.

Equally important were the observation posts (OP) in the surrounding countryside. Bloc PL 19 was a concrete bunker located at Hallembaye. It incorporated three machine guns and an armoured observation dome. Its crew

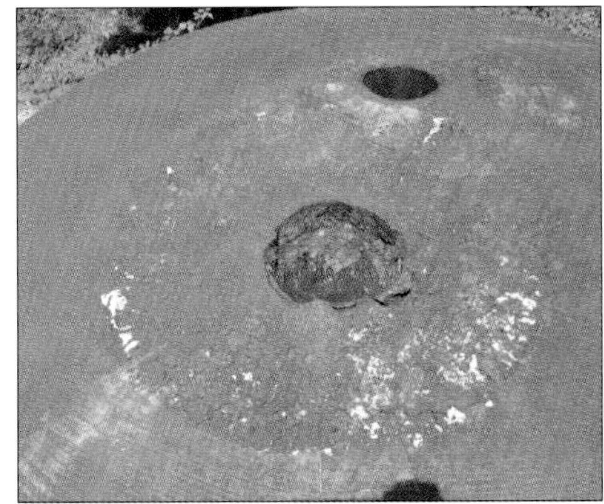

The armoured observation domes of Fort Eben Emael were well situated with wide fields of view. For this reason they were the priority targets for Sturmgruppe Granit. In the foreground is EBEN 2 atop Mi-Nord, with its line of sight overlooking the Albert Canal towards Maastricht. Although this photograph was taken soon after the battle, the damage caused by a 50kg hollow charge has already been disguised by filling the hole with concrete so as to preserve the secret of the *Hohlladungwaffe* for as long as possible. After the battle, numerous visitors from the German armed forces and foreign representatives were given guided tours of Fort Eben Emael to mark the outstanding feat of arms of Sturmgruppe Granit. In the background is the crucifix marking the spot where the dead of Sturmgruppe Granit were buried. The close-up photograph shows the actual damage to EBEN 2 as visible today. Although there was no penetration, the shock wave caused steel splinters and scabs to detach at high velocity from the interior surface, killing and wounding those inside. Above the damage is the circular slot for a periscope down which Feldwebel Wenzel jammed a 1kg charge that wounded the observer in the initial attack.

Besides the gun emplacements, an anti-tank ditch and further anti-tank obstacles in the form of reinforced concrete 'dragons' teeth', together with extensive barbed wire entanglements to deter infantry attack, protected the eastern and southern sides of Fort Eben Emael. These can be seen here below Bloc 01 overlooking the Albert Canal and Meuse River to the north-east of the fortress. The armoured observation dome EBEN 1 is shrouded beneath camouflage netting, as were all the positions prior to the German assault. From inside the dome, an observer could see all the way to the German border, and it was from here that the only effective fire missions of Coupole Sud and Visé 2 were controlled, as well as those of other forts to the south. Bloc 01 was separated from the main fortress by over 100m and the Germans never attacked it. Just minutes before the surrender of Fort Eben Emael, Private Ferdinand Ancia, volunteered to demolish the position, which he achieved by detonating an explosive charge in the connecting tunnel of Galerie 01. Tragically, he died in the explosion, and he was the last casualty of the battle for Fort Eben Emael. The colour photograph shows the field of view from EBEN 1 across the Albert Canal and the Lanaye locks into Holland and on to the German border. (Photos Centre de Documentation historiques des Forces armées and Simon Dunstan)

comprised four NCOs, and 14 soldiers. Facing the strategic bridge over the Albert Canal at Kanne was the emplacement ABRI 0 with a 47mm anti-tank gun, a machine gun, a searchlight, and an armoured observation dome. It had a crew of three NCOs and nine soldiers. There were an additional six observation posts, although these were in unprotected positions, each with three personnel. All eight of these OPs were connected by telephone with the command post at Fort Eben Emael. There were also 14 foxholes dotted around the highest points of the fort, each with two armed men who also acted as observers for the fortress itself. In times of high alert, they were to be equipped with field telephones to communicate with the command post in case of attack or suspicious movement.

The garrison

The full complement of the garrison was 1,322 men under the command of an artillery major. Many of these were support and administrative personnel responsible for the smooth running of the fortress, including specialist armourers, signallers, and medical staff. The actual gun crews were all artillerymen and consequently had little infantry training. During World War I, every fort had its own complement of infantry, but, due to manpower shortages, this precaution had lapsed during the inter-war period. For administrative simplicity the artillerymen were divided into two batteries – 1er Batterie and 2e Batterie. The personnel of 1er Batterie manned the long-range artillery while the 2e Batterie was responsible for the perimeter defences. The garrison rotated its personnel on a weekly basis so at any one time there were approximately 750 men in the fortress. However, what with leave, courses, illness, et al, the complement was often less. Some half of the garrison were obliged to sleep inside the fort's cramped and dank interior, with the remainder billeted in the surrounding villages, the majority at Wonck some 4km away. For the same reason, a pair of large wooden buildings was constructed just outside the entrance at Bloc 1 to house the administrative staff and the command element in more agreeable surroundings. In time of war, the buildings were to be evacuated and razed to the ground so as not to impede the fields of fire of Blocs 1 and 2.

In all, there were some 5km of underground galleries and tunnels to serve the totally self-sufficient garrison. On foot, it took 20 minutes to reach Bloc 01 from the entrance at Bloc 1, 14 minutes to Mi-Nord, 13 minutes to Coupole Nord, seven to Coupole Sud, and nine minutes to reach the MICA anti-aircraft position over the top of the fort. To visit every position took some three hours of walking. The fortress comprised in all some 17 powerful gun emplacements with ten on top and seven around the perimeter. As one Belgian officer, Colonel Albert Torreele, recalled of a visit from the Ecole Royale Militaire in 1938:

> An officer of the garrison of the fort led us to many of the outer defences and showed what each was intended for. We went to the walls and looked over the countless rows of barbed wire. He led us to the only door on the surface set deep in concrete. It appeared like the heavy steel door of a bank vault. From here [Coupole Nord] infantry in reserve would issue to repel any enemy fortunate enough to get by the tough ground defences.
>
> He took us deep into the interior and we trudged many miles to the end of the tunnels, visiting the crews and the guns of the emplacements we had seen on the surface. Crews gave us their missions and detailed characteristics of their guns. All was very professional. Later, we assembled in the command post. The commandant gave a detailed account of how he proposed to defend the fort in the event of an attack. I got the impression of tremendous power and first-rate efficiency. I was convinced nothing could happen!

By now Fort Eben Emael had gained a formidable reputation, as the famous American journalist and historian William L Shirer, wrote at the time: 'This modern, strategically located fortress was regarded by both the Allies and the Germans as the most impregnable fortification in Europe, stronger than anything the French had built in the Maginot Line or the Germans in the West Wall.'

With almost 5km of underground tunnels and galleries connecting the various gun emplacements, resupply within Fort Eben Emael was a major task. Ammunition was transported in handcarts from the ammunition magazines to the gun emplacementsd by means of hoists, or in an emergency by hand up the stairwell. On the right is a 75mm ammunition cart and on the left a water bowser.

Fall Gelb – Case Yellow

The strength of Fort Eben Emael was vexing the German High Command (*Oberkommando der Wehrmacht* or OKW) following the conquest of Poland in September 1939. In a lightning campaign that gave rise to the term blitzkrieg, the German Army introduced a new concept in warfare as an answer to the predominantly positional fighting of World War I. It was now apparent that the British and French were not prepared to withdraw from the war and allow Adolf Hitler to remain master of central Europe. The Führer insisted that OKW devise a plan, codenamed *Fall Gelb*, for the invasion of France in the autumn of 1939 to forestall further Allied preparations. The first concept was based on the Schlieffen Plan, with the main thrust into Belgium north of Liège following the path of von Gluck's First Army of 1914. A force of some 37 divisions (Army Group B) was to be deployed on this front with a secondary strike of 27 divisions (Army Group A) to the south through the Ardennes region of Belgium. Thanks to the Maginot Line, this was exactly what the Allied commanders expected. Fundamental to the French strategy was to avoid hostilities in the Lille/Cambrai region of north-east France, where two-thirds of her coal reserves lay and the source of her industrial power. The only solution was to take the fight to the Germans on Belgian territory once they had invaded the country and violated her neutrality.

To this end, it was essential to the Allies that the Belgian Army and the *Position Fortifiée de Liège*, with Fort Eben Emael at the crucial juncture, delay the German Army for sufficient time to allow Allied forces to deploy into Belgium. But because of Belgian neutrality, there was virtually no coordination between the respective armies as to a concerted defence plan, let alone with the Dutch, who remained fearfully vulnerable to German invasion. Both Belgium and Holland realized that they lay in the path of a German invasion of France, but deceived themselves into believing that a policy of strict neutrality would forestall the inevitable. As the months passed by, all the western powers facing the threat of Nazi invasion squandered valuable time on useless and pusillanimous static defence lines that paid no regard to the concept of blitzkrieg. To the various western high commands, the German triumph over Poland was due to the weakness of the Polish armed forces rather than a novel form of warfare.

Accordingly, the Allies first devised Plan E whereby they would advance into Belgium as far as the Scheldt River but, after months of inactivity that the British press termed 'sitzkrieg', a bolder Plan D emerged that called for an advance as far as the Dyle River, a few miles east of Brussels. With the British defending the upper Dyle, the Belgian Army was to fall back on the Albert Canal to protect Antwerp, with Fort Eben Emael at the hinge, while the French were to hold the strategic Gembloux Gap between the Dyle and the Meuse rivers. It was to this area that the French Supreme Commander, Général Maurice Gamelin, assigned his strongest formations, with the mechanized First Army under Général Georges Blanchard and the Seventh Army of Général Henri Giraud to act in support of the Dutch. Thus the best of the French army was to be deployed to a foreign country while its weakest elements, the Second and Ninth Armies, were committed to the area opposite the Ardennes Forest that the French High Command believed to be impassable.

The German preparations for an invasion of the west in November 1939 were thwarted by bad weather. A bitterly cold winter ensued with the date of the attack postponed to 17 January 1940. However, one week before the appointed day, a Luftwaffe plane strayed off course and was forced down in Belgium. Inside were the plans for the air phase of the coming invasion. They confirmed the French assessment that the German invasion was to come through the Liège area of Belgium and not the Ardennes region. The Allies were put on high alert with French forces moving to their assigned sectors along the border regions. None was allowed to cross into Belgium because of her adherence to neutrality. German observers were quick to note the French dispositions and the weakness of the forces around Sedan. At the behest of Adolf Hitler, the OKW was instructed to revise *Fall Gelb*. At the instigation of Lt. Gen. Erich von Manstein, the chief of staff to Col. Gen. Gerd von Rundstedt, the commander of Army Group A, and Maj. Gen. Heinz Guderian, the commander of XIX Panzer Korps, *Fall Gelb* was fundamentally changed with the major attack, the *Schwerpunkt*, now to be undertaken by a heavily reinforced Army Group A through the Ardennes region. It was a risky proposition but Hitler was persuaded. The offensive was postponed due to bad weather and the need to redeploy the necessary forces. In the north, Army Group B, commanded by Col. Gen. Fedor von Bock, was reduced to 28 divisions, of which only three were armoured. Army Group A was enlarged to 44, with seven of them being Panzer divisions. Once through the Ardennes, they were to drive full tilt for the English Channel, trapping the Belgian, British and French armies in Belgium.

Nevertheless, for *Fall Gelb* to work, it was essential to entice the mobile forces of the Allies into Belgium and they were unwilling to move unless Belgian and Dutch neutrality was violated. To achieve this, Army Group B was to invade Holland and seize the road and rail bridges over the Meuse River at Maastricht and then, some 10km beyond the city, the three road bridges over the Albert Canal. These were located at Veldwezelt, Vroenhoven and Kanne. If they were captured intact, the heartland of Belgium lay open to the German Army. If they were destroyed, the Sixth Army of Gen. Walter von Reichenau would be trapped inside the Maastricht enclave at the mercy of the guns of Fort Eben Emael. The whole success of *Fall Gelb* depended on the capture of these strategic bridges and to do that Fort Eben Emael, the strongest fortress in the world, had to be neutralized.

Sturmabteilung Koch

By the terms of the Versailles Treaty, Germany was denied an air force. With the rise to power of the Nazi party and Adolf Hitler in 1933, numerous fliers were trained through the use of gliders that were not part of the ban, as the Allies did not realize their military potential. By the late 1930s, Germany had numerous world champions in the 'sport' of gliding, including the famed aviatrix Hanna Reitsch, Hitler's favourite pilot. It was the Führer himself who found the answer to the assault on Fort Eben Emael. With mopping-up operations still continuing in Poland, Hitler summoned Lt. Gen. Kurt Student, the commander of the recently created paratroop formation, the 7th Flieger Division, to the Reichs Chancellery on 27 October 1939. Under the control of the Luftwaffe, the 7th Flieger Division was the world's first fully operational airborne division. (See Osprey Battle Orders 4: *German Airborne Divisions: Blitzkrieg 1940–41* by Bruce Quarrie, Osprey: Oxford, 2004)

Consideration had been given to employing paratroopers of the division in an airborne assault on Fort Eben Emael but there were severe reservations. The slow-flying Ju52 transport planes carrying the paratroopers would be highly vulnerable to Dutch and Belgian anti-aircraft guns, even on the short journey from Germany to the target. Furthermore, despite its large size, it was estimated that too few paratroopers could land on the top of Fort Eben Emael as many would be dispersed by the wind and other factors – a stick of paratroopers jumping from a Ju52 in seven seconds at the minimum operational flight would commonly be spread over an area of 300m. Even if they did land in

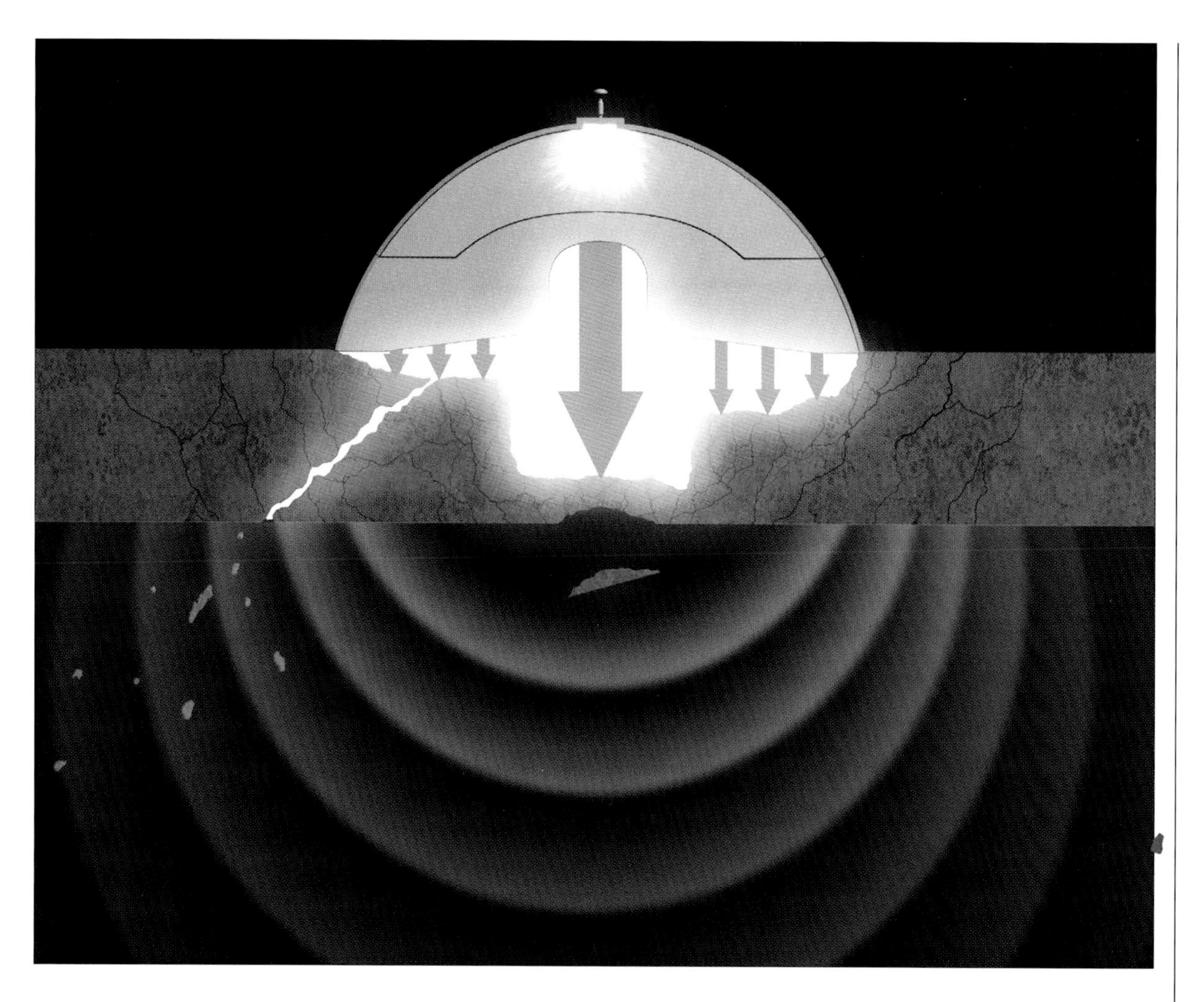

***Hohlladungwaffe* – hollow-charge explosive**

The shaped or hollow-charge explosive principle was discovered in 1888 by an American, Charles Edward Munroe and it has become known as the 'Munroe Effect'. In 1910, it was improved by a German scientist named Egon Neumann. A Swiss chemical engineer, Henry Mohaupt, further refined the idea in the late 1930s and offered it to the French army, which was due to accept a hollow-charge anti-tank weapon on exactly the same day that the Germans first used their own version in anger, 10 May 1940. The largest 50kg *Hohlladungwaffe* came in two parts for easier handling by two men. The 50kg charge was delicate and any damage could result in a lesser explosive effect, which was one reason why they were delivered by glider rather than parachute. Also any damage to the seal between the two halves diminished the penetrative force significantly. Nevertheless, the *Hohlladungwaffen* proved highly effective on the day both militarily and psychologically. The priority targets were the armoured observation domes on the various gun emplacements. Although none was fully penetrated by the detonations, the blast and 'spalling' from fragments being detached from the interior surface of the domes were sufficient to kill and injure the Belgian observers and render the positions useless. The spalling effect and blast overpressure are shown to good effect in the artwork. The charges were also used to gain entry into the reinforced concrete gun emplacements by the assault pioneers of Sturmgruppe Granit. Thereafter, the remaining charges were used against targets of opportunity that further demoralised the Belgian garrison with their awesome destructive power.

Born on 14 August 1916, Rudolf 'Ralf' Witzig enlisted in April 1935 and joined the 16th Pionierbataillon. He was commissioned in April 1937, and in October 1938 qualified as a parachutist. Because of his engineering skills, Oberleutnant Witzig was chosen by Hauptmann Walter Koch to lead the pioneer assault against Fort Eben Emael. It was through his rigorous training regime that Sturmgruppe Granit proved to be such an effective fighting force despite his absence at the outset of the attack. Through sheer determination, he obtained another Ju52 to rescue his stranded DFS 230 and tow it, together with Trupp 11, to Fort Eben Emael. For the triumph of Sturmgruppe Granit, Oberleutnant Rudolf Witzig was awarded the Ritterkreuz and promoted to Hauptmann. He subsequently fought in Crete, Tunisia and on the Eastern Front. He ended the war as a major fighting on the Western Front, after which he spent several months in captivity. In January 1956, he joined the newly created Bundeswehr and ended his career as a full colonel on the staff of the Pioneer School in Munich. Rudolf Witzig died in October 2001. (National Archives and Records Administration)

sufficient numbers, the question remained as to how lightly armed paratroopers could destroy the heavy fortifications.

With remarkable tactical acuity, Hitler recognized the one potential flaw in the defences of Fort Eben Emael. He demanded to know from Gen. Student whether the Luftwaffe's combat glider, the DFS 230, was capable of landing on the grassy roof of the fortress. As a pioneer glider pilot himself, Student pondered for 24 hours and returned to the Reichs Chancellery to inform the Führer that he believed it would be possible to land up to 12 gliders but only in daylight or, at worst, in twilight. However, he remained uncertain as to how 80 to 90 paratroopers were to destroy the gun emplacements. It was then that Hitler revealed the existence of a new weapon that had been developed in great secrecy – the *Hohlladungwaffe* or hollow-charge weapon. Produced in various sizes, with the heaviest weighing 50kg, German scientists believed that these hollow-charge weapons were capable of breaching the fortifications of Fort Eben Emael. Hitler then gave Gen. Student a direct order to capture the fortress and the three bridges over the Albert Canal that were vital to Hitler's offensive in the west. It was to be the first airborne glider assault in military history.

Gen. Student immediately created a new, highly specialized unit under the command of Hauptmann Walter Koch, which gave rise to its name of Sturmabteilung Koch. Calling for volunteers for a hazardous mission, he selected ten other officers and 427 other ranks, including 42 glider pilots. Most of the troops came from the 1st Battalion of the 1st Flieger Regiment (I/FJR 1), with the addition of a platoon, or Zug, from the Pionierkompanie of II/FJR 1. The latter were assault pioneers under the command of Oberleutnant Rudolf Witzig and consisted of one other officer, Leutnant Egon Delica, and 83 other ranks. They were given the most important task of neutralising Fort Eben Emael.

Within days of Hitler's operational order, Sturmabteilung Koch began training on 3 November 1939 at Hildesheim, near Hannover, under the conditions of the utmost secrecy. For this reason, Koch's unit was initially designated Experimental Section Friedrichshafen, and the name changed periodically, while Witzig's assault pioneers were given the title Airport Construction Platoon. Feldwebel Helmut Wenzel, the senior NCO in the platoon, recalled:

> We couldn't go into bars, but we could go to movies. However, we had to have a guard. Usually by the time the movie was over, the guards had lost interest and gone home ... Also we didn't wear insignia and we had other names. Once we ran into some girls we knew and the whole unit had to be transferred.

Every man was required to sign a confidentiality form stating: 'I am aware that I shall risk sentence of death should I, by intent or carelessness, make known to another person by spoken word or illustration anything concerning the base at which I am serving'. Two enlisted men were indiscreet with some local girls on one occasion. They were arrested, charged, court-martialled, and sentenced to death within 24 hours.

Such was the secrecy that Witzig's men never actually witnessed the detonation of the hollow-charge weapons until they took them into action at Fort Eben Emael. Training was done with mock-up weapons of the same weight as the real ones. This was undertaken at captured fortifications at Gleiwitz in Poland, and on the Czech Benes Line near Sumperk in the Sudetenland. There they practised assault techniques against casemates and gun emplacements using all their other weapons, including Bangalore torpedoes, flamethrowers and conventional explosive charges. Although they knew neither the name nor the location of the target, they were aware of its configuration thanks to *Sankastelmodells*, or sand table models, and the layout of the various gun emplacements was also taped out using measurements derived from aerial reconnaissance pictures.

By March 1940, Sturmabteilung Koch was trained to a high pitch. It was now designated No. 17 Reserve Squadron and was divided into four groups – three to capture the bridges and one to neutralize Fort Eben Emael. Each was given a suitable codename with Sturmgruppe Stahl (Steel) to assault the bridge at Veldwezelt to the north; Sturmgruppe Beton (Concrete) the bridge at Vroenhoven; Sturmgruppe Eisen (Iron) the one at Kanne; and Sturmgruppe Granit (Granite) for the attack on Fort Eben Emael. The success of the whole operation was predicated on the ability of the Luftwaffe to land the assault troops in close proximity to their targets. Sturmgruppe Stahl was composed of nine gliders carrying one officer and 91 men; Sturmgruppe Beton had 11 gliders with five officers and 129 men including the command element of Haupt. Koch; Sturmgruppe Eisen had ten gliders with two officers and 88 men while Sturmgruppe Granit had 11 gliders with two officers and 84 men, but with an extra glider because of the weight of the hollow-charge weapons and the other assault equipment.

Each group was subdivided into squads with one squad per glider. As manpower was so limited, all the glider pilots were trained in assault tactics and the use of the various demolition weapons. The pilots were drawn from the airlanding element (17./KgrzbV 5) of the 7th Flieger Division. The 42 DFS 230 gliders and pilots were each assigned their own towing aircraft of a Ju52 'Tante Ju'. Each glider and Ju52 became a dedicated team and all flight training was done together so that a *glucklich Verheiratet* or 'happy marriage' was formed between the aeroplane and glider pilots in the difficult task of formation flying at night. However, trials of glider landings on a simulated area of Fort Eben Emael revealed that the DFS 230 required a longer stopping distance than was available, especially when landing on wet grass that was only to be expected with the dawn dew. Modifications were made by incorporating a wooden drag brake beneath the glider that dug into the ground on landing.

Flügkapitan Hanna Reitsch conducted a test flight that was almost her undoing as the brake proved only too effective. On landing she was slammed into the control column, and only her foresight to protect her chest with an extra parachute saved her life. Further modifications solved the problem but

The paratroopers of the 7th Flieger Division wore a distinctive uniform of a jump smock and a different helmet to the classic German Stahlhelm. As all their weapons were dropped in separate containers, all paratroopers carried a pistol as a personal firearm for their immediate defence on landing. The standard pistol was the 7.65mm Sauer Modell 38H, or, later, the 9mm Walther P38. These were issued to glider troops as well, and the pistol holster is seen here on the equipment belt of Gefreiter Eddi Schmidt of Trupp 4. Beside him is Oberjäger Ernst Grechza of Trupp 5, who disgraced himself by becoming intoxicated during the attack after filling his water canteen with rum. There is no record of Grechza being injured during the action, so his bandaged head remains a mystery; either it was a self-inflicted wound through drunkenness, or else he might have got on the wrong end of Fw. Wenzel's fist for his antics. Ernst Grechza was killed in action on the island of Crete in 1941. Eddi Schmidt survived the war and died in 1991.
(Photo Centre de Documentation historiques des Forces armées)

The principal defence of Fort Eben Emael against air attack was the MICA position located at the south-eastern end of the fortress; MICA standing for *mitrailleuse contre avions*. It comprised four machine-gun pits around a central command position, all interlinked by deep trenches. As anti-aircraft weapons, the machine guns were configured for firing skywards but they could also fire across the surface of the fortress as a further counter to infantry attack. In the event, two machine guns jammed without firing, one was knocked over by the wing strut of a DFS 230, and the other fired approximately 50 rounds before the position was overrun by the men of Trupp 5 under the command of Feldwebel Haug. (Fort Eben Emael)

another had arisen. The difficult approach path and limited landing area of Fort Eben Emael was proving too problematic for many of the Luftwaffe pilots of 17./KgrzV 5. Koch turned for advice to his glider specialist, Walter Kiess, and the designers, Deutsches Forschungsinstitut für Segelflug, whose expert test pilots quickly proved that such a landing was feasible in a fully laden DFS 230. Many of the pre-war champion glider pilots were 'invited' to provide their expert services to the Reich with such internationally known names as Bredenbeck, Braütigam, Lange and Raschke being coopted into Sturmgruppe Granit. Two full-scale dress rehearsals were conducted and many of the pilots were now able to land and stop their aircraft within 20m of their assigned targets.

Those for Sturmgruppe Granit were carefully selected to maximize the limited quantity of men and resources that could be carried by 11 gliders. The primary objectives were those gun emplacements that were capable of engaging the three bridges across the Albert Canal. These were Maastricht 1 and 2 that the Germans designated *Werk*, or Objectives, 12 and 18 respectively, followed by Coupole 120, or Objective 24, and Coupole Nord, or Objective 31. Coupole Sud, or Objective 23, was a supplementary target as it was believed by the Germans to be incapable of firing on the bridges to the north. However, the first priority was to destroy those emplacements that could disrupt the assault landing itself. These included the MICA anti-aircraft machine guns, Objective 29, as the gliders were highly vulnerable to small arms fire and the two machine-gun casemates Mi-Nord and Mi-Sud that could slaughter exposed troops in the open. These became Objectives 19 and 13 respectively. Interestingly, the two false cupolas at the northern tip of the fortress were also primary targets and these were designated Objectives 15 and 16 – a rare instance of faulty German intelligence. The 11 squads of Sturmgruppe Granit were cross-trained to attack each other's targets should one squad be incapacitated. All of them had supplementary targets and tasks once their primary mission was accomplished. The crucial elements to the offensive striking power of the fortress were the observation domes on Mi-Nord (EBEN 2) and Maastricht 2 (EBEN 3), which could direct the artillery against the vital bridges to the north. Without them, the guns would be blind. It was the task of Sturmgruppe Granit to pluck out the eyes of Fort Eben Emael.

The other side of the hill

By May 1940, Sturmabteilung Koch was straining at the leash for the coming offensive, but the situation for the defenders of Fort Eben Emael was very different. Since the outbreak of war eight months before, the morale of the garrison of Fort Eben Emael had plummeted. The bitter winter of 1939/40 had made conditions inside the dank fortress most unpleasant. The inferior quality of the cement lining the interior tunnels was causing it to crumble with the result that many of the garrison were suffering from chest infections from the dust. In January 1940, the garrison was redesignated as the 1er Groupe within the Régiment de Fortresse de Liège, comprising 1er and 2e Batteries. However, the garrison was so undermanned that personnel were drawn from several of the other forts around Liège. But, in a long military tradition, the men ordered from one unit to another were invariably the least efficient or, at worse, malcontents. Furthermore, fortress duty was much less attractive than serving in the field artillery so the calibre of the personnel, particularly officers, was often lower. The garrison commander himself, Major Jean Fritz Lucien Jottrand, tried to have his appointment to Fort Eben Emael on 26 June 1939 reversed as his home was in Brussels. Of the 28 other officers, 17 were reservists and only one career officer, Captain Hotermans, had served in the fort since it was built. Nine others arrived from April 1939 onwards and Lt. Desloovere, responsible for Visé 1 and 2, only arrived on 2 May 1940. None had any infantry training, and of the 20 revolvers specified for the reserve officers only four were available.

During the previous months there had been several general alerts but they had all been false alarms. These occurred on 11 November 1939, 10 January 1940 and 10 and 14 April 1940. Each time leave for the garrison had been cancelled, damaging morale further. There had also been regular alerts that were exercises as part of general training. Another failing of Fort Eben Emael was that it was far from any town so there was no form of entertainment for the troops during their off-duty hours. All the other forts were closer to towns and cities such as Visé or Liège, with tramlines and bus routes nearby. For the garrison of Fort Eben Emael, there was nothing to do in the village after which it was named or in the dormitory village of Wonck. On the evening of Thursday, 9 May 1940, the fortress chaplain received several complaints when the night's film showing was cancelled, but at least five-day leave passes had been restored and many were making plans for a break from garrison duty. Due to illness and other factors, the number of troops available in the fortress that night was well below that necessary for waging war. Major Jottrand had 211 men in his command and administrative staff; 271 men of 1er Batterie under the command of Capt. Vamecq to man the artillery casemates and cupolas; and 507 men of 2e Batterie under Capt. Hotermans to man the perimeter defences: a total of 989 men, with 230 of them on stand-by at Wonck some 4km away.

But these were the least of the problems for Fort Eben Emael. As part of the *Position Fortifée de Liège*, the fortress came under the command of 3e Corps for administrative purposes with its headquarters in Liège. However, in November 1939, 1er Corps took over responsibility for the region north of Fort Eben Emael, including the three bridges over the Albert Canal. Whereas Fort Eben Emael was connected to 3e Corps via a dedicated military telephone network, as well as the vulnerable civilian one, 1er Corps relied on wireless transmission for communications with the fortress, as well as the civil telephone network, but by chance Fort Eben Emael had a chronic shortage of trained signallers. Accordingly, secure communications between the fortress and the surrounding units it was supposed to support and receive fire missions from in combat were patchy at best, and had never really been put to the test. Unlike most European armies, the Belgian military did not have a telex system. Although all the bridges over the Albert Canal were mined, those at Vroenhoven and Veltwezelt were the responsibility of an officer at the area headquarters at Lanaken. Only he could give the order for their destruction by the prepared demolition charges.

Major Jottrand was charged with the destruction of the bridge at Kanne to prevent it falling into enemy hands, as well as those at Petit Lanaye and the canal locks. He was not allowed to destroy the two bridges over the Geer River that were just outside the fortress as these came under the command of 3e Corps. The situation was exacerbated by the overly complex command and control structure for the guns of Fort Eben Emael. These were required to be coordinated with the field artillery regiments and batteries of the surrounding units. Of these, the 2e Grenadiers Régiment of the 7e Division d'Infanterie that was to the immediate north of Fort Eben Emael had only arrived on 2 May 1940. However, it was responsible for 2.4km of the Albert Canal to the north of Fort Eben Emael and 4.5km of the canal to its south, but the regiment was forbidden to enter the grounds of the fortress including the 1.3km length of the canal through the Caster cutting.

Thus, Fort Eben Emael was supposed to support the units of the 7e Division d'Infanterie to its north and south as well as the left flank of 3e Corps that was

At 0830hrs on 10 May 1940, four hours after the attack on Fort Eben Emael began, the German ambassador presented himself at the Belgian Foreign Ministry. Before he could speak, the Belgian foreign minister, M. Paul Spaak, interjected – 'I beg your pardon, Mr. Ambassador. I shall speak first,' and in an indignant voice he read the Belgian Government's protest, 'Mr Ambassador, the German army has just attacked our country. This is the second time in 25 years that Germany has committed a criminal aggression against a neutral and loyal Belgium. What has just happened is perhaps even more odious than the aggression of 1914. No ultimatum, no note, no protest of any kind has ever been placed before the Belgian Government. It is through the attack itself that Germany has violated the undertakings given by her on 13 October 1937 and renewed spontaneously at the beginning of the war. The act of aggression committed by Germany for which there is no justification whatever will deeply shock the conscience of the world. The German Reich will be held responsible by history. Belgium is resolved to defend herself. Her cause, which is the cause of Right, cannot be vanquished.' In 18 days, the German Army crushed Belgium. Belgian neutrality had failed again. (National Archives and Records Administration)

designated Secteur Meuse-Aval. Whereas formerly, all the guns came under the control of the Groupements d'Artillerie de Campagne du 3e Corps, they now came under the command of various disparate units with Coupole 120 controlled by Est d'A/CA du I.C.A; Coupole Nord and Sud by 7e Division d'Infanterie; Maastricht 1 and 2 by 18e Régiment d'Infanterie de Ligne; Visé 1 by 2e Grenadiers Régiment; and Visé 2 by Secteur Meuse-Aval. To complicate matters further, the 12e Régiment d'Artillerie, supporting the 7e Division d'Infanterie and coordinating the fire missions of Fort Eben Emael, was replaced by the artillery regiment of the Chasseurs Ardennais on 24 April 1940. Its personnel were all French speaking whereas those of the 7e Division d'Infanterie and Fort Eben Emael spoke mainly Flemish. A language barrier now compounded the problems of poor wireless communications.

Major Jottrand's tactical command was further proscribed by secret orders signed by the chief of staff himself that he had received personally from two staff officers from 1er and 3e Corps respectively on the evening of 14 April 1940. These explicitly forbade him from firing the guns of Fort Eben Emael into Dutch territory, even if foreign troops entered Holland or the Dutch requested Belgian support. This was to comply with the strict terms of Belgian neutrality that the government still maintained was in the best interests of the country, even after the conquest of Poland and the invasions of Denmark and Norway by the Germans. Through a combination of manpower shortage, poor morale, inefficient communications and political interference, the strength of the most powerful fortress in the world was being seriously undermined, but worse was to follow.

The alert

At 1900hrs in the evening of 9 May 1940, the military attaché of the Belgian embassy in Berlin, Lt. Col. Goethals, informed the Belgian High Command that the Germans were on a war footing and would invade next day. This followed earlier warnings from the Dutch military attaché in Berlin, and even Pope Pius XII himself, that the Germans were about to attack. On 7 May, a French pilot returning from a leaflet-dropping mission over Dusseldorf reported sighting a 60-mile-long German armoured column advancing on the Ardennes. Yet the Belgian High Command did not issue a general alert until 2230hrs on 9 May. It did not arrive at HQ 3e Corps until 0025hrs, and 1er Corps 30 minutes later. Fort Eben Emael was warned at 0030hrs. Major Jottrand arrived at his command post at 0100hrs followed by the commander of 2e Batterie, Capt. Hotermans, at 0120hrs and the commander of 1er Batterie, Capt. Vamecq, at 0150hrs. But information from the outside world remained sparse. Indeed, there was none from the Belgian High Command for several hours as the general staff moved to its wartime headquarters.

As part of a general alert, it was standard operating procedure for one of the 75mm cupolas to fire a pre-arranged number of blank rounds in a set sequence, 20 rounds 30 seconds apart divided between the four points of the compass, to summon the remainder of the garrison from their quarters and to warn the field units in the surrounding countryside. At 0055hrs, Coupole Nord was ready to fire the warning shots, but an order came from higher command to wait. The commander of Fort Aubin-Neufchateau received a similar instruction, but it has never been discovered who gave these orders. They were to have decisive and tragic consequences. Nevertheless, a runner was sent to warn the other garrison troops at Wonck but it took time to rouse the men from all the different lodging places, and many were only aware of the alert when Fort Eben Emael began belatedly to fire the warning shots.

Arguably, the fate of Fort Eben Emael was directly attributable to the two buildings outside the main entrance of Bloc I that were completely separate from the fortress. Of all the unfortunate circumstances that led to the fall of Fort Eben Emael, it was Major Jottrand's order to have the outside administrative buildings emptied and demolished that had such disastrous consequences. As there were too few men in the garrison, many members of the crews manning the gun emplacements were recalled to Bloc I to undertake the task, leaving the casemates severely undermanned, and, in the case of Mi-Sud, empty. In addition, the men from the 14 fighting foxholes dotted around the top of the fortress were all brought back to Bloc I, so there were no observers on top of the fortress at the time of the German attack. If they had been in position, there was every likelihood that the gliders would have been spotted sooner, giving the defenders more warning. But then again, each of the foxholes was supposed to be equipped with a field telephone connected to the command post, but they had been lent to a camp at Helchteren. In the event, neither of the buildings was demolished in time, and most of the damage visible here was sustained during Stuka attacks. It begs the question that if these buildings had to be demolished at the time of an attack alert why this had not been done in any of the previous four alerts. (Photo Centre de Documentation historiques des Forces armées)

At 0200hrs, Maj. Jottrand gave a seemingly innocuous yet fateful order when he instructed the two wooden administrative buildings just outside Bloc 1 to be evacuated and all material moved into the fortress. As a methodical officer, Maj. Jottrand was simply following standing orders that in case of attack, the two buildings were to be emptied and then razed to the ground so as not to compromise the fields of fire of Blocs 1 and 2. Because the warning shots had not been fired to summon the troops from the outlying villages, there were insufficient men to do the job. Accordingly, the gun crews from Coupole Nord, as well as Mi-Nord and Mi-Sud, and the observers in the 14 foxholes atop the fort were recalled to Bloc 1 to undertake the task. Further men were summoned from other casemates. With the exception of Mi-Sud, all the other observation domes were manned from the outset of the alert. Major Jottrand also contacted his eight observation posts outside the fortress and ordered the demolition charges on the various bridges to be primed.

Finally, the order to fire the warning shots was given at 0230hrs. Maj. Jottrand passed the instruction to the officer of the day, Capt. van der Auwera, who in turn passed it to Lt. Verstraeten in charge of the 75mm cupolas. Unfortunately there were now too few trained men at Coupole Nord to undertake the mission as most of the gun crew were demolishing the administrative buildings. The fire mission was passed to Coupole Sud but nothing happened. During an earlier exercise, the firing pins of the 75mm guns had been removed and by some oversight not replaced. An armourer had to be found and bring new ones from the stores behind Bloc 1, causing a further delay. Yet Maj. Jottrand was not overly concerned. No German troops had invaded Holland and even when they did it would take time for them to cross the Meuse River and arrive on Belgian territory. There was still time for the administrative buildings to be levelled and the gun crews to return to their emplacements. At 0325hrs, some three hours after the original alert, Coupole Sud began to fire, but after only a few rounds the camouflage netting shielding the armoured cupola caught fire, obscuring the gunner's periscope. The cupola commander ordered three men to extinguish the fire and clear the optics of the periscope. This interrupted the pre-arranged firing sequence of the warning shots causing confusion among many troops in the field, including some of the garrison personnel at Wonck.

It was now 0335hrs and the last of a strange armada of aircraft was lifting off from airfields in Germany. At Fort Eben Emael, Coupole 120 reported that it was having difficulties with its ammunition hoists and it was unable to fire, but the almost complete gun crew was working on the problem. The gun emplacement was also lacking an important periscope. At Coupole Nord, only

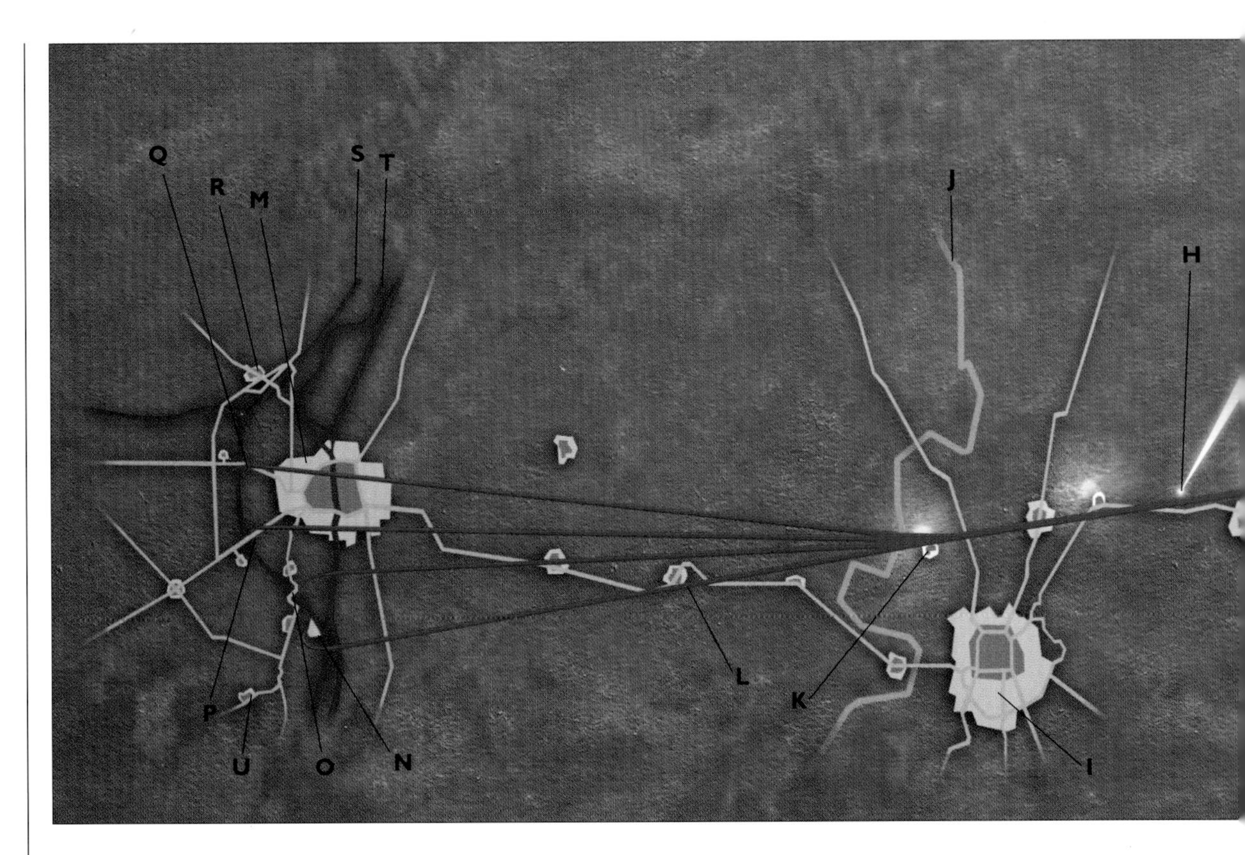

13 of the gun crew were present but of these none were qualified gun layers and the emplacement was not yet ready for action. After firing its interrupted warning shots, Coupole Sud had most of its gun crew and was ready for action, but it did not have any 75mm canister rounds available. At Visé 1, 11 of the 32-man crew were missing. Visé 2 was almost complete with 29 out of 32. The gun crew of Maastricht 1 had been stripped to provide men to clear the administrative buildings and only seven men remained, which was insufficient to man the guns. In addition, the periscope for the observation dome EBEN 3 was missing. At Mi-Nord there were just one NCO and four soldiers out of a gun crew of 21. That was far too few to man the four machine guns and the two searchlights. Furthermore, they had been forbidden to break open the ammunition cases and load the machine guns. The ammunition came in sealed boxes to preserve it from deterioration and once opened they could only be resealed by specialized armourers. During a previous alert, the commander of Bloc 6 had opened some ammunition cases and been castigated for doing so. However, the three observers of EBEN 2 were present, but they had not fitted the periscope in the observation dome. At night, it tended to get obscured by condensation so no one thought to install it despite the alert. At Mi-Sud, there was not a single member of the gun crew as they were all at Bloc 1 demolishing the administrative buildings. The perimeter defences were generally undermanned, with only Canal Sud having a full complement. At the MICA anti-aircraft position, only 19 out of the 27-man gun crew were in position at the four machine-gun mounts. Furthermore, the hand grenades they were issued had no fuses so were useless. Other members of the gun crew were sheltering in the MICA hut nearby waiting for the end of the alert.

'The sun shines red, be ready'

On the afternoon of 9 May 1940, Sturmabteilung Koch assembled on the airfields of Köln-Ostheim and Köln-Butzweilerhof near Cologne. Each of the

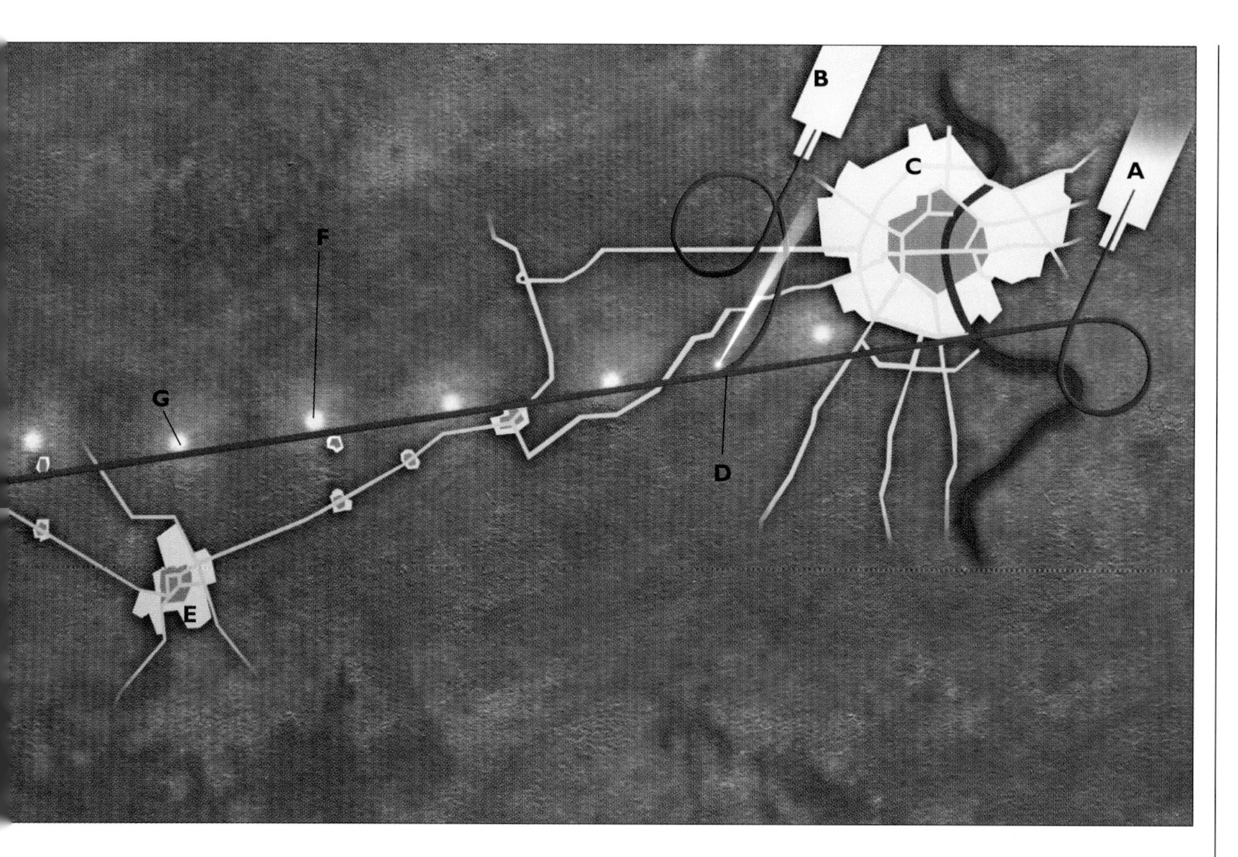

Flightpath

On Friday 10 May 1940, the air operations of Sturmabteilung Koch required 42 gliders and their attendant Ju52s as well as six additional Ju52s to drop an extra 73 Fallschirmjäger at the bridges, 24 at Veldwezelt, 24 at Vroenhoven and 25 at Kanne, some 40 minutes after the initial glider landings. Three gliders aborted with two belonging to Sturmgruppe Granit but one of these arrived later containing Lt. Rudolf Witzig, the commander of Sturmgruppe Granit. This diagram shows the flight path of the assault force from the airfields of Köln-Butzweilerhof and Köln-Ostheim with the series of bonfires and searchlights that indicated the route to the Dutch border. Ten Ju52/DFS 230 combinations took off from Butzweilerhof and 32 from Ostheim including the 11 gliders of Sturmgruppe Granit. The rallying point was around the first searchlight pointing vertically into the air close to the village of Frechen. The line of beacons was a combination of huge bonfires, rotating lights and vertically pointing 60cm anti-aircraft searchlights that were illuminated for 30 seconds and then extinguished for ten seconds; the sequence being repeated throughout the flight. With the rest of Germany lying in pitch darkness because of the wartime blackout, the lights were readily visible to the aircrew. The distance between Köln and Aachen was 72km and the air flotilla was to reach the release point for the gliders at a height of 2,600m (8,500ft) in 32 minutes at a speed of 140km/hr but due to a strong tail wing, it took longer than expected to climb to the designated altitude so the actual release point was over Dutch territory rather than north-west of Aachen as planned. Once released, the gliders achieved a speed of 124km/hr at a glide angle of 1:12 to travel the average distance of 27km to the targets in just under 14 minutes. The first glider landed on Fort Eben Emael at 0424hrs Belgian time, which was one hour behind German or Central European Time.

KEY

A. Ostheim aerodrome
B. Butzweilerhof aerodrome
C. Cologne – Köln
D. Rallying point near Efferen
E. Düren where the glider of Trupp 2 landed
F. Bonfires on flightpath
G. Rotating lights on flightpath
H. Vertical pointing searchlights on flightpath
I. Aachen – Aix-la-Chapelle
J. Border of Germany and Holland
K. Proposed release point for gliders
L. Actual release point for gliders over Gulpen
M. Maastricht
N. Fort Eben Emael
O. Kanne bridge
P. Vroenhoven bridge
Q. Veldwezelt bridge
R. Lanaken
S. Albert Canal
T. Meuse River
U. Wonck

gliders was loaded with almost a ton of equipment and explosives. Everything was carefully lashed down and secured to prevent it from shifting in flight and upsetting the critical centre of gravity of the gliders or else injuring the paratroopers. At 2130hrs, the sealed orders were opened and the troops informed of the targets they were to attack after their months of intensive training. For the next few hours, Luftwaffe ground crew prepared and positioned the Ju52s with their respective DFS 230 gliders. The towing cables and release mechanisms were checked time and again. Reveille for the paratroopers was set for 0145hrs from whatever rest they were able to achieve. After a final briefing and the issue of the stimulant methedrine to each man, the paratroopers boarded their gliders by squad. Corporal Wilhelm Alefs of Squad 7 recalled the final minutes before takeoff:

> It was very black. I felt around and found the explosives and everything else as it should be and as I left it five hours earlier. I patted the pockets of my jacket to feel the grenades, then the ones above to see if my machine pistol ammunition was there, unconscious but reassuring gestures. I reached into the pocket of my inner jacket to feel the fuse and cord for the explosives. The glider began rocking as the pilots of the tow planes revved the engines whose roar was muffled to us in the now tightly closed glider. We didn't take off at once. There were many other planes and gliders to take off ahead of us, and it was those I could hear power up as they went down the runway. Suddenly, a jerk on the glider forced me backwards. There was a jockeying and sloshing motion as the towrope tightened and swung the glider behind the straining plane ahead. Simultaneously, we all started the chant of the paratroopers – 'Rot Scheint die Sonne, fertig gemacht.'

Ten Ju52/DFS 230 combinations took off from Köln-Butzweilerhof and 32 from Köln-Ostheim, including the 11 gliders of Sturmgruppe Granit. It took longer than expected to get all the aircraft airborne and the last glider carrying Witzig's Trupp 11 did not take off until 0335hrs. As they moved into formation, it was apparent that the Trupp 5 glider was wallowing badly putting undue strain on the towrope, but once its Ju52 gained sufficient speed it flew normally. All the gliders were loaded to or above their nominal capacity and it took time to reach the necessary altitude of 2,600m (8,500ft) and the release point just to the north-west of Aachen. The air armada was guided on its way by a series of large bonfires on the ground interspersed with anti-aircraft searchlights pointing vertically into the sky. The pilot of one Ju52 recalled that the line of bonfires resembled a long necklace of sparkling rubies. The paratroopers in the dark and freezing bellies of the gliders had no opportunity or inclination to admire the view. As the aircraft passed 1,000m, disaster struck

The ability of the DFS 230 to make a pinpoint landing is clearly shown here with this glider that came to rest just 50m from the western end of the bridge at Veldwezelt. The bridge itself was just beyond the houses in the background, with the main Maastricht to Antwerp road running between the buildings. The *estaminet* (pub) on the right was blown up by German engineers as part of the bridgehead defences. Of particular interest is the lack of national markings on the fuselage and tail of the DFS 230. This was a deliberate *ruse de guerre* by the Germans to confuse the Belgian defenders and gain precious moments during the vulnerable final approach to the targets. It can be seen clearly that the Balkenkreuz on the side of the fuselage has been overpainted to disguise the national identity.
(Photo Centre de Documentation historiques des Forces armées)

as the towrope of Witzig's glider snapped when its Ju52 abruptly banked to avoid colliding with another aircraft. With no possibility of reaching Fort Eben Emael, Witzig ordered his pilot to land the glider to the east of the Rhine in German territory. Unteroffizer Pilz tried manfully to nurture the heavily laden glider back to base but it came down 6km short of Ostheim. After ordering the paratroopers to prepare a rudimentary airstrip, Witzig ran to the nearest village where he commandeered a vehicle and returned to Ostheim where he arrived around 0405hrs. There was not a single Ju52 available but the duty officer summoned one from Gütersloh to be put at Witzig's disposal.

Unaware of this calamity, the air armada flew on when disaster struck again. For some unaccountable reason, the pilot of the Ju52 towing the glider of Trupp 2 signalled to its pilot, Unteroffizer Bredenbeck, to separate even though they were only at an altitude of 1,600m. Realising this was a mistake, Bredenbeck refused, but when the Ju52 began to waggle its wings and dive to force the DFS 230 loose, he was obliged to unhitch. The glider began an unscheduled descent over German territory, landing near the town of Düren. Within the space of a few minutes, Sturmgruppe Granit was reduced to 70 men without a shot being fired in anger. But they soon were. Due to a strong tailwind, the air armada arrived at the release point at 0400hrs. This was earlier than planned and as yet not at the correct height to allow the gliders to fly all the way to Fort Eben Emael. The Luftwaffe flight commander sensibly decided to gain more altitude even though this meant flying into Dutch air space. As the formation did so, it came under fire from Dutch anti-aircraft batteries, but the fire was desultory and inaccurate although disconcerting inside the flimsy, canvas-covered gliders. It did, however, alert the Belgians to the impending attack. After a further ten minutes flying time, the Ju52s reached the requisite altitude of 2,600m and all the gliders were released without mishap. With a glide slope of 1:12 and an airspeed of 124km/hour, the gliders required just 12 minutes to fly the 27km to the targets.

The first glider assault in warfare

Sturmabteilung Koch was scheduled to land at its targets at 0425hrs, just five minutes before the launching of *Fall Gelb* and Hitler's offensive in the west. At the same time, the road bridges across the Meuse River at Maastricht were to be captured in a coup de main by a special Abwehr unit (Bau-Lehrbattalion zur besonderen Verwendung 100) but it failed and the bridges were blown up by their Dutch defenders, although a railway bridge was taken intact at Maaseik in Belgium. This mishap was to upset dramatically the German timetable with significant consequences for Sturmabteilung Koch, which was now swooping down on its targets. From north to south, the action unfolded with varying degrees of success. At the Veldwezelt bridge, Sturmgruppe Stahl (Oberleutnant Gustav Altmann and 91 men in nine gliders) landed at 0420hrs under heavy fire. The glider of Trupp 9 was hit and lost part of its wing as well as wounding the pilot in the head. The DFS 230 plunged to the ground from a height of 10m, injuring all but two men on board. Due to ground fog visibility was poor, causing Trupp 6 to land some 1,000m away and the other gliders were dispersed but sufficient troops were at hand to complete the mission with the destruction of the

Sturmgruppe Stahl captured the bridge at Veldwezelt intact at a cost of eight dead and 30 injured. Soon after landing, the paratroopers attacked Bunker N on the western side of the Albert Canal, visible here at the end of the bridge in the background. The 12 occupants of the bunker from the Escadron des Cyclistes-Frontière du Limbourg were killed outright. Beneath the bridge, built into the pile, was Bunker C, which was also attacked with explosives, trapping those inside. Early in the evening of 10 May, the first elements of the 4th Panzer Division arrived at the bridge and the first tanks to cross, shown here, were from the 2 Zug, 6 Kompanie of Panzer Regiment 36, commanded by Oberstleutnant Jesser. The men caught inside Bunker C were from the 6e Compagnie of the 2e Carabiniers. They were not released until 1100hrs on the following day, when the distorted door was prised open by German engineers. Over the next few days, the Belgian, French, and Royal air forces mounted bombing raids against the captured bridges. On 12 May, No.12 Squadron, Advanced Air Striking Force, undertook a mission. Flying slow and vulnerable Fairey Battle bombers, four of the five aircraft that attacked the Veldwezelt bridge were shot down, but Flying Officer Donald Garland and his observer, Sergeant T. Gray in P2204 PH-K, were posthumously awarded the first RAF Victoria Crosses of World War II. (National Archives and Records Administration)

defensive bunkers and the disabling of the demolition charges. This was achieved within ten minutes. Sturmgruppe Stahl then dug in at each end of the bridge to defend their prize. With Stukas on hand providing fire support, two machine-gun teams were dropped by parachute at 0515hrs under fire from the Belgian defenders. One soldier was killed during the drop, one was injured and one parachute failed to open. The two teams landed some distance from the bridge but were able to bring effective fire on the Belgians as they began to mount counter-attacks with the strongest occurring at 0800hrs. This was broken by a combination of defensive fire and Stuka dive-bombers. The Germans defending the bridge then came under artillery and mortar fire, but this was soon answered once radio contact was made with Flak-Abteilung Aldinger and its 88mm Flak guns. German reinforcements arrived during the course of the afternoon and the bridgehead was expanded westwards. At 2030hrs, Sturmgruppe Stahl withdrew from the bridge and returned to Germany via Maastricht. It had captured the vital Veldwezelt bridge at a cost of eight dead, 14 severely wounded, and 16 lightly wounded; a casualty rate of over a third. Belgian casualties were 110 dead and approximately 200 prisoners.

The significance of the high bridge over the Albert Canal at Vroenhoven can be appreciated from these photographs. If it had been demolished, along with the similar high bridge at Veldwezelt, it would have taken considerable time and engineer effort for the Germans to replace them with approach roads down to the canal sides and pontoon bridges across it.

Sturmgruppe Beton was under the command of Leutnant Gerhard Schacht, and comprised 11 gliders with five officers and 129 men, including Maj. Koch's command element. However, one glider failed to reach the target after its towrope parted and it was forced to land at Hottdorf. The remainder came under fire over Maastricht but no casualties ensued. At 0415hrs, the gliders landed under fire from the defenders. The glider of Trupp 8 was hit on its final approach and the control wires were cut, causing it to crash from a height of 12m, badly injuring three men. The paratroopers charged towards the bridge and its defensive bunkers. Gefreiter Stenzel was the first to arrive and burst through the open door just as the demolition charges were being ignited. With great presence of mind, he cut the wires and the bridge was saved. As Lt. Schacht had landed 1,200m to the west of the bridge, Oberfeldwebel Hoffmann, whose squad had suffered several casualties, now commanded the assault force. Houses close to the bridge were destroyed to provide clear fields of fire as a pair of machine-gun teams were dropped by parachute to reinforce Sturmgruppe Beton. One man was killed and another drowned when he plunged into the Albert Canal. The two machine guns were then set up to support the three squads at each end of the bridge. Meanwhile, Maj. Koch set up his headquarters and established contact with his other units as well as VIII Flieger Korps. Stuka support and the guns of Flak-Abteilung Aldinger contained Belgian counter-attacks. Further reinforcements arrived during the afternoon and early evening when Belgian heavy artillery tried to destroy the bridge without success. At 2040hrs hours, Sturmgruppe Beton withdrew from the scene of their victory. The cost was seven dead and 24 wounded, while the Belgians suffered 147 dead and about 300 prisoners.

As one of the observation posts of Fort Eben Emael, Bloc 0 overlooked the Kanne bridge across the Albert Canal. It was manned by three members of the garrison, and was armed with one 47mm anti-tank gun and one machine gun. On the orders of Maj. Jottrand, the bridge was blown up as the gliders of Sturmgruppe Eisen landed nearby. Later in the day, the men of Trupp 2 of Sturmgruppe Granit under the command of Oberjäger Maier arrived at Kanne. After their glider had landed in Germany, Maier had commandeered some trucks and drove through the advancing columns of the German Army to get to Fort Eben Emael as quickly as possible. Trupp 2 captured 121 Belgian prisoners of war, but Maier would not hand them over without a receipt to prove that he had done everything in his power to complete his mission. Tragically, Oberjäger Max Maier did not live to see the victory of Sturmgruppe Granit as he was killed during the fierce fighting in Kanne on 10 May, but he was buried with his comrades on the heights of Fort Eben Emael. (National Archives and Records Administration)

Unlike the other sites, the assault at Kanne presented particular problems for Sturmgruppe Eisen, as there was no suitable landing ground for gliders close to the bunker (Bloc 0) guarding the bridge. Under the command of Lt. Martin Schächter, Sturmgruppe Eisen comprised ten gliders carrying two officers and 88 men, but the glider of Trupp 1 was released too soon and landed on the heights south-west of the bridge where it was unable to effect the battle. Ground fog masked the position and the remaining gliders landed at varying distances from the target. The DFS 230 of Trupp 3 was hit and caught fire on its final approach, while Trupp 9 came down 200m to the south near the village of Eben Emael.

The Belgian observers inside Bloc 0 watched transfixed as the gliders bumped to a halt, but quickly contacted Maj. Jottrand inside Fort Eben Emael for instructions. He gave the decisive order to destroy the bridge, and within moments the single steel span collapsed into the canal. Despite this setback, Sturmgruppe Eisen continued the attack against the Belgian bunkers and trenches. The fierce fighting continued sporadically throughout the day with Belgian counter-attacks at 0930hrs, 1400hrs and 1700hrs. German reinforcements from Infanterie Regiment 151 arrived at 2230hrs to support the bridgehead, but there was no relief for Sturmgruppe Eisen until the early morning when they withdrew to the east bank of the canal. They had suffered severe casualties of well over 50 per cent, with 22 dead, 26 wounded and one missing in action. The Belgians losses were 216 dead, 50 wounded and 190 prisoners of war.

The assault of Sturmgruppe Granit

The capture of two out of the three bridges was a triumph by any measure of success, but it would have been for naught if the guns of Fort Eben Emael

The gliders of Truppe 5 and 8 were the first to land on Fort Eben Emael, with the DFS 230 of Trupp 8 touching down at 0424hrs in the first glider-borne assault in the history of warfare. While the men of Trupp 8 attacked Coupole Nord, Trupp 5 tackled the MICA anti-aircraft position. This can be seen to the left of the photograph, with the DFS 230 of Trupp 5 in the middle and that of Trupp 8 to the right. In the foreground is the anti-tank ditch, and behind the glider of Trupp 8 was the Graindorge barracks. This building housed the personnel that maintained and repaired the various weapons of Fort Eben Emael. To the left of the photograph, the wooden MICA hut is just visible on the skyline. It contained two spare machine guns. Ironically, it was these two weapons firing from a wooden structure that caused the first German fatalities of the assault rather than the purpose-built machine-gun emplacements of Mi-Nord and Mi-Sud. (Photo Centre de Documentation historiques des Forces armées)

The chaplain of Fort Eben Emael, L. Meesen, kept a diary of events that give an interesting insight into the atmosphere inside the fortress at the time of the attack:

'Thursday, 9 May 1940. The news is good tonight – five-day leave passes have been reinstated. The troops are making plans. As for me, I have decided to take three days off between 20 and 23 of May … Around 9 o'clock, we go back to the fort. Not knowing what to do at the village many soldiers are returning as well. The news about the restoration of leave is spreading. Once again everything is going extremely well … Half past twelve at night. We are woken up by the sound of a bugle and pandemonium in the galleries. It's the alarm. Is it real this time or will it be another drill again? And what about our leave? The outcome of each alert has always been the cancellation of leave for an unspecified length of time … Everything is quiet. No sound or light from the village. As with every other alarm everything from the outside buildings has to be moved into the fort – officers' mess, records and files. The men are working willingly. Nobody is expecting a war. Some of them however, thinking of their leave, are working reluctantly … I intend to go back when I am told that twenty gunshots will be fired from Coupole 120 [sic]. This seems to be getting serious. Could this really mean war? The major [Jottrand] has been told that the turret is not working. An act of sabotage? I believe the shots will be fired from another cupola [Mi-Sud]. At that time I reached my room inside the fort and I couldn't hear the twenty shots being fired … Father Lamaye who did not leave comes to see me around four thirty - "We are at war!" he says "German planes have landed on the fort." So it is real this time. I put my helmet on, take my gas mask and we go out into the passage … The men are bustling about everywhere. What is going on above us? … I am going to the infirmary. Our three doctors are there, Commandant Willems and Lieutenants Dumay and Steegen. Doctor Steegen tells us that he has seen planes coming down onto the fort. The machines were flying silently, their engines stopped. Yet at that time we didn't know they were planes without engines – gliders!'

remained intact. As dawn broke, the fortress was shrouded in a light mist, but its distinctive diamond shape was readily discernible to the glider pilots as they circled overhead at a height of 300m losing altitude the while. The command post was informed of their approach from several of the observation posts outside the fort, but Maj. Jottrand was at Bloc 1 supervising the clearing of the administrative buildings. Adjudant Longdoz also saw the circling aircraft and ran to the telephone at the MICA barracks for instructions. Longdoz was under the impression that the aircraft were British reconnaissance aircraft and the command post told him not to open fire until their nationality was established, but at that moment Capt. Hotermans gave the order to engage the intruders. By now the gliders of Sturmgruppe Granit were on their final approach, and by the time the MICA anti-aircraft guns opened fire, it was too late.

Two of the four guns jammed immediately, and only a few short bursts were fired before the DFS 230 of Trupp 5 swept in so low that its wing brace smashed one of the machine guns as it came into land. In all only 50 rounds were fired by the MICA, but German reports later indicated that six of the nine gliders were hit by machine-gun fire on landing, although no casualties occurred. It is probable that the gliders suffered many hits in the ensuing battle. Within moments, the paratroopers of Trupp 5 rushed the position with grenades and overwhelmed the defenders, most of whom were taken prisoner. One Belgian soldier was killed and another mortally wounded. The delay engaging the gliders when they were at their most vulnerable was a critical failure, as was the order given by Capt. van der Auwera at 0420hrs, minutes before the gliders landed. If the top of the fortress was under threat, the correct command was to sound the alert – *Attaque massif* but instead van der Auwera sounded *Attaque générale,* which indicated a general attack from the surrounding countryside. With *Attaque massif,* the standing operating procedure was for all the machine guns to be manned and loaded, while the 75mm guns of the casemates and cupolas were to be primed with canister rounds to engage any infantry in the open. None of the gun emplacements therefore had canister rounds to hand and the machine-gun ammunition remained sealed in its boxes.

By now the nine remaining DFS 230 gliders of Sturmgruppe Granit had landed and most of them had succeeded in stopping with remarkable accuracy close to their targets. It must be appreciated that all the actions related below happened simultaneously. Since the original alert, most of the crew of Maastricht 2 had returned to the casemate including the observers of EBEN 3, Maréchaux des logis David and Marchoul. The position was commanded by Maréchal des logis Poncelet. However, the ammunition hoists had failed and no one had seen fit to carry any rounds up to the guns via the staircase. After a bumpy landing, Trupp 1, under the command of Feldwebel Niedermeier but with Lt. Egon Delica, the Luftwaffe air liaison officer, to hand, ran to their target – Objective 18 (Maastricht 2). Niedermeier carried one half of a 50kg hollow-charge weapon and Gefreiter Drucks the other half. This they assembled over the armoured observation dome, EBEN 3, and initiated the ten-second fuse before scrambling for cover. The ensuing explosion failed to

The remains of the DFS 230 of Trupp 7 lie broken on the north-western edge of Fort Eben Emael. The glider pilot, Unteroffizier Heinz Scheithauer, and Gefreiter Wilhelm Höpfner were severely injured during the landing and took no further part in the fighting. Behind the glider are the remains of one of the false cupolas that Trupp 7, under the command of Oberjäger Fritz Heinemann, destroyed soon after landing. The other false cupola, complete with dummy guns, that appeared identical to Coupole 120, was the target for Trupp 6. These false cupolas were mounted on a rotating ballrace so that their aspect could be altered to confuse aerial reconnaissance. This serious lapse of German intelligence wasted the efforts and resources of two whole squads, or almost 25 per cent of the landing force, at a critical juncture of the battle. The DFS 230 was designed and built by the Deutsches Forschungsinstitut für Segelflug, hence the designation DFS. It first flew in 1937 and 1,022 were built by Gothaer Waggonfabrik between 1938 and 1941. It comprised a lattice of steel tubes covered with fabric to form the fuselage, and a high shoulder-mounted plywood wing. With an unladen weight of 860kg, it had a maximum take-off weight of 2,100kg, although those of Sturmabteilung Koch were probably overloaded and this caused some towropes to break. The DFS 230 cost just 7,500 Deutsche Marks, which was equivalent to the price of ten RZ16 parachutes of the time. 10 May 1940 was the first time that gliders were used offensively in warfare. (Photo Centre de Documentation historiques des Forces armées)

penetrate the heavy armour but the blast overpressure killed the two occupants. The gun position filled with fumes and the lights failed. Another explosion followed shortly when a 12.5kg charge was detonated below the left hand 75mm gun, causing it to be blasted back off its mounting. Privates Ferire and Phillipe were killed outright and Brigadier Verbois mortally wounded. Hand grenades were thrown through the opening, wounding more men, and the Belgians withdrew down the stairwell to the intermediate level below. Niedermeier and two other paratroopers then entered the casemate and immediately donned gas masks because of the fumes. After passing a wounded Belgian soldier out into the fresh air, the squad took up guard by the stairwell to ward off a Belgian counter-attack. The glider pilot, Feldwebel Raschke, placed a swastika flag above the position to indicate to Luftwaffe aircraft that the position was taken. Maastricht 2 had fallen, and with it its triple 75mm guns pointing northwards to the bridges over the Albert Canal. Of the Belgian gun crew of 24, four were dead and 17 wounded, some with severe burns and smoke inhalation. Two telephonists were trapped in their booth by the displaced 75mm gun and were only released on the following day. The Belgians inside the fortress sealed off the position with the barrier of metal beams and armoured doors.

Maastricht 1 was the target for Trupp 3 under Oberjäger Arendt. Their glider had made a textbook landing, stopping just 25m above and to the east of the objective, as the casemate was built into the hillside overlooking the Geer River. At the time there were just seven Belgian soldiers inside; some sources suggest ten. They were under the command of Maréchal des logis Gigon. Attempts by Trupp 3 to attach a 50kg charge against the face of the casemate failed, so a 12.5kg was wedged under the left-hand 75mm gun. The resulting explosion killed Private Bormans and wounded several others. Although wounded himself, Gigon manhandled two of his comrades down the many steps to the level below. He then donned a gas mask and returned to the smoke-filled gun room to help the other wounded, but the toxic fumes forced him back. Shortly afterwards, some of the paratroopers entered the casemate, where they captured three wounded Belgians. They then threw hand grenades down the stairwell, which cut off the electricity supply. The position was plunged into darkness. The Belgians had no alternative but to seal off the position behind the barrier of steel beams and armoured doors. Only one member of the Belgian gun crew remained uninjured. Those that could, staggered off to the hospital, where they found the burnt and battered survivors of Maastricht 2. The two vital northern-facing gun emplacements guarding the bridges of Veldwezeldt and Vroenhoven were now in German hands.

Both Truppe 6 and 7 were assigned targets at the very northern end of the fortress where its tip pointed towards Maastricht. Designated by the Germans as Objectives 14 and 16 respectively, they were two large domes identical to Coupole

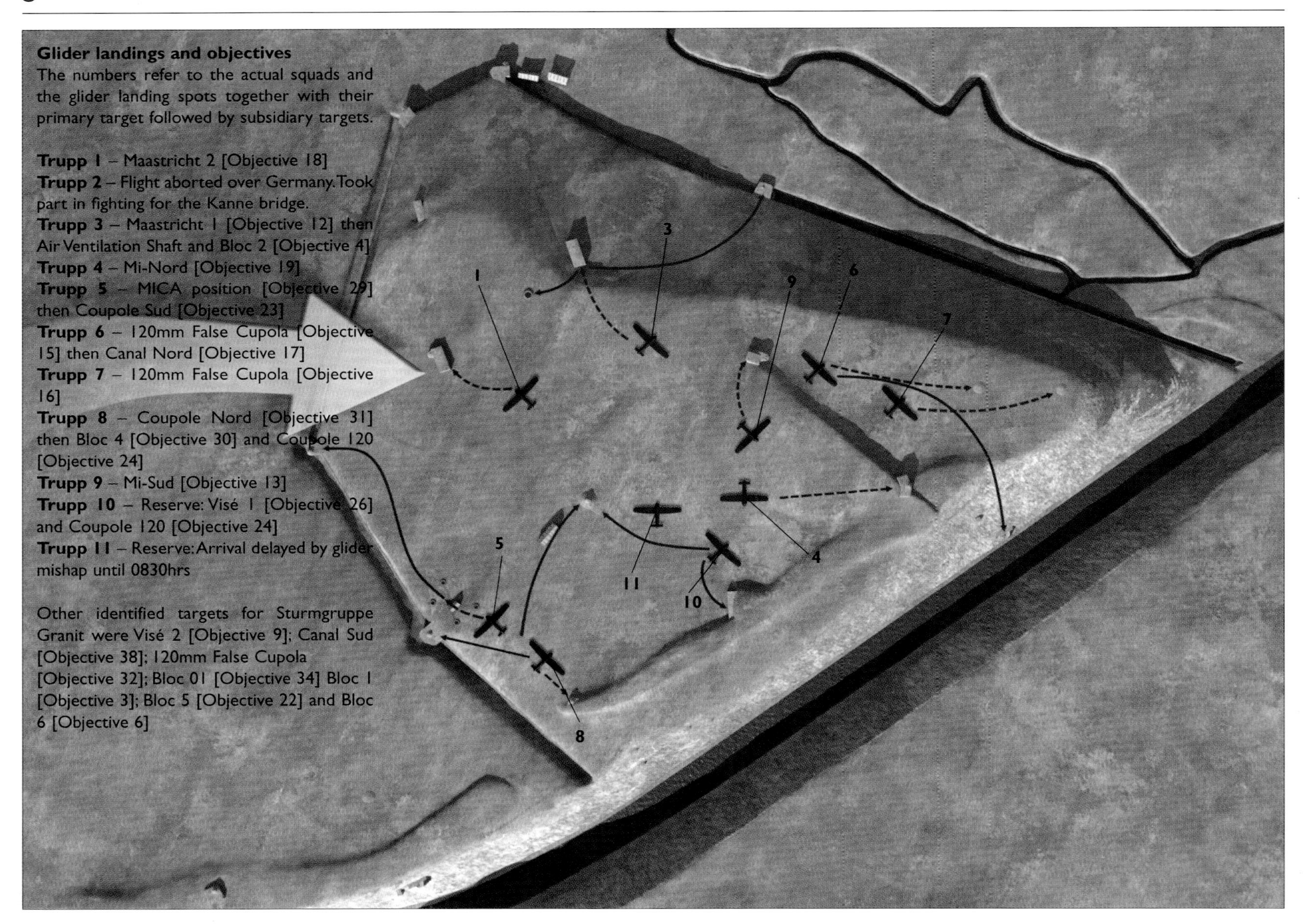

Glider landings and objectives
The numbers refer to the actual squads and the glider landing spots together with their primary target followed by subsidiary targets.

Trupp 1 – Maastricht 2 [Objective 18]
Trupp 2 – Flight aborted over Germany. Took part in fighting for the Kanne bridge.
Trupp 3 – Maastricht 1 [Objective 12] then Air Ventilation Shaft and Bloc 2 [Objective 4]
Trupp 4 – Mi-Nord [Objective 19]
Trupp 5 – MICA position [Objective 29] then Coupole Sud [Objective 23]
Trupp 6 – 120mm False Cupola [Objective 15] then Canal Nord [Objective 17]
Trupp 7 – 120mm False Cupola [Objective 16]
Trupp 8 – Coupole Nord [Objective 31] then Bloc 4 [Objective 30] and Coupole 120 [Objective 24]
Trupp 9 – Mi-Sud [Objective 13]
Trupp 10 – Reserve: Visé 1 [Objective 26] and Coupole 120 [Objective 24]
Trupp 11 – Reserve: Arrival delayed by glider mishap until 0830hrs

Other identified targets for Sturmgruppe Granit were Visé 2 [Objective 9]; Canal Sud [Objective 38]; 120mm False Cupola [Objective 32]; Bloc 01 [Objective 34] Bloc 1 [Objective 3]; Bloc 5 [Objective 22] and Bloc 6 [Objective 6]

120 from the air. They were in fact the dummy positions known to the Belgians as Coupoles 1 and 2. German intelligence had been in error, belying later allegations that they had the complete plans of the fortress. The glider of Trupp 6 under the command of Oberjäger Harlos skidded to a halt in the barbed wire entanglements behind the earth rampart connecting Mi-Sud with Mi-Nord. For some minutes, the paratroopers had difficulty leaving the glider because the wire was jamming the exit. The DFS 230 lay stranded between the two gun emplacements and at the mercy of Mi-Sud's machine guns, but no fire came. Once out of the glider, the paratroopers rushed towards their objective only to discover it was a dummy position that had already been destroyed by Trupp 7. Accordingly, Harlos set up his MG34 machine gun close by in a position that dominated the northern end of Fort Eben Emael. Trupp 7 under Oberjäger Heinemann had made a heavy landing, badly injuring the pilot, Unteroffizer Scheithauer, and Gefreiter Höpfner. The glider came to a halt in the open close to the two false cupolas and the remainder of the squad destroyed them both in short order. Thus the efforts of 16 paratroopers were wasted on the destruction of two sheet steel structures. Furthermore, because of their position at the northern end of the fortress behind the earth rampart running between Mi-Sud and Mi-Nord, they were effectively cut off from the rest of Sturmgruppe Granit and played no real part during the height of the assault.

The museum at Fort Eben Emael contains many interesting artefacts including these hollow-charge weapons, or *Hohlladungwaffen*, and explosive charges as used by Sturmgruppe Granit during the assault on the fortress. On the left is the two-piece 50kg charge with the leather carrying handles and the fuse at the top. Beside is the compact H12 *Hohlladungkörper* 12.5kg hollow-charge weapon that proved so effective against the triple 75mm gun emplacements. The other two devices are standard explosive demolition charges in 3kg and 1kg sizes. Feldwebel Wenzel used the latter type in his initial attack on EBEN 2 of Mi-Nord, while the 3kg charge was used to great effect to destroy stairwells to prevent Belgian counter-attacks against the captured gun emplacements.

As the first glider over Fort Eben Emael, the DFS 230 carrying Trupp 8 of Oberjäger Unger made a spectacular final approach after its pilot, Unteroffizer Distelmeier, flew below the level of the eastern wall of Fort Eben Emael to avoid any anti-aircraft fire, pulling up at the last moment over the anti-tank ditch and landing just 25m from the objective, Coupole Nord. Deep below ground, the gun crew of Coupole Nord had observed the gliders landing and immediately informed the command post. Severely undermanned, the acting commander of the cupola, Maréchal des logis Joiris, acted on his own initiative and ordered his ammunition handlers to collect canister rounds from the magazine for the 75mm guns. At the critical moment, the ammunition hoists failed to work. Undaunted, Joiris ordered the rounds to be carried up the stairs, but as they were being loaded into the guns a massive explosion occurred. Oberjäger Unger had just detonated a 50kg *Hohlladungwaffe* on the armoured dome of Coupole Nord. Almost immediately, there was another explosion as a 12.5kg shattered the steel grille and armoured door of the infantry exit. The detonation also destroyed the ammunition hoists that had been repaired by the armourer, Brigadier Biesmans. He was killed by the blast and four others were wounded. Another 50kg hollow charge was detonated on top of Coupole Nord at 0445hrs. Although neither of the two charges penetrated the armoured carapace, the shock waves of the explosions damaged the rotation mechanism of the cupola and the electricity supply, rendering Coupole Nord ineffective. The Belgians withdrew to the intermediate level and sealed off the position. Another threat to the Albert Canal bridges had been eliminated.

Meanwhile, the fighting near the MICA position continued unabated with the Germans suffering their first fatalities. After overrunning the anti-aircraft machine guns, Trupp 5 went to the assistance of Trupp 8, but both squads came

Stuka dive-bombers repeatedly attacked the main entrance to Fort Eben Emael at Bloc I, causing considerable superficial splinter damage to the face of the casemate. Direct-fire weapons, mainly 37mm PaK anti-tank guns that were concealed near the watermill on the Geer River facing Bloc I, caused most of the damage around the gun embrasures. This view shows the northern aspect of Bloc I with the 60mm anti-tank gun at the bottom, the machine-gun embrasure above, and the searchlight housing to the right. At the top left are the steps that gave access to the top of the fortress. In another excerpt from the chaplain's diary, this one from Friday afternoon, 'Through the periscope of Bloc I's machine gun, many soldiers can be seen arriving in twos and threes at the front gate of the fort from Wonck. They are being let in and arrive, totally deadbeat. It took them three, four hours along a road that they would normally take them 30 minutes. All along the way, they have suffered bombing and strafing … I go to the gate to welcome those who are coming in. Some are weeping from exhaustion. As soon as they get in, they fall to the ground in a heap, refusing to move … I settle them down and tell them to rest for a few hours. For the time being no one knows what to do with them anyway and besides, they are unable to do anything at the moment.' (Fort Eben Emael)

under fire from the MICA hut. Trapped inside the wooden building since the gliders landed, Adjudant Longdoz had erected the two spare machine guns and was directing their fire against the German paratroopers Jäger Meyer of Trupp 8 was wounded in the shoulder as he assaulted Coupole Nord. Once the latter had been subdued, the men of Truppe 5 and 8 mounted an attack on the position but suffered two killed – Truppführer Unger and Obergefreiter Bögle of Trupp 5. Using their Belgian prisoners of war as a shield, the paratroopers advanced towards Bloc 4, which overlooked the anti-tank ditch running along the south-eastern edge of Fort Eben Emael. Once there, a 50kg hollow charge was detonated above the armoured observation dome of Bloc 4 killing Private Furnelle. One by one the eyes of Fort Eben Emael were being plucked out with deadly precision.

The DFS 230 of Trupp 9 came to rest close to the barbed wire entanglements fronting Mi-Sud. Led by Oberjäger Neuhaus, the paratroopers of Trupp 9 had to use wire cutters to approach the gun emplacement, whose armoured shutters remained ominously closed. Under sporadic machine-gun fire from the MICA position to the south-east, they inched their way forward while a flamethrower operator prepared to pour liquid fire into the gun embrasures should they be opened. Once at Mi-Sud, attempts were made to attach a 12.5kg charge to the gun embrasure but without success, so a 50kg charge was then lodged against the machine-gun embrasure and detonated, blowing it apart. Trupp 9 took up defensive positions inside Mi-Sud. The position had fallen without firing a shot as the casemate was empty. When alerted by the attack the gun crew rushed to the position just as the first 50kg charge detonated. There was nothing else to be done except seal off yet another gun emplacement from the interior of the fortress.

The other machine-gun casemate, Mi-Nord, proved to be equally impotent despite being manned. Its machine guns remained hidden behind their armoured shutters and, worse, there was no ammunition to hand. It was still in its sealed boxes. As a pre-war world-record gliding champion, Unteroffizer Brautigam's landing was not as smooth as expected, and the DFS 230 of Trupp 4 came to a halt some 80m short of Mi-Nord. The Truppführer, Feldwebel Wenzel, grabbed some explosive charges and rushed the position followed by two Oberjägers, Köhler and Florian, each carrying one half of a 50kg hollow-charge weapon. Wenzel clambered up the earth rampart beside Mi-Nord and jammed a 1kg charge down the vacant periscope housing of the armoured observation dome, EBEN 2. It will be recalled that the optical device had not been fitted inside EBEN 2 by the observers because of early morning condensation. The blast of the explosion vented through the opening and injured the observer, Maréchal des logis Bataille. As his companions rushed to his aid, a far larger explosion followed as a 50kg hollow charge was detonated on top of EBEN 2. Although it did not pierce the dome's thick armour, the shock wave killed Bataille and Maréchal des logis Vossen outright, and severely injured Maréchal des logis Diricks as well as wounding other soldiers inside the casemate. With relentless determination, Trupp 4 continued their assault on the gun emplacement by detonating a 12.5kg charge at the left-hand machine-gun embrasure followed by another 50kg charge that blasted a large hole in the wall of the casemate. With the electricity cut and the interior filled with smoke and flame, the Belgians

retreated to the intermediate level and sealed off the position. The defenders had not fired a single shot. The two gun emplacements whose sole purpose was to defend the top of the fortress against ground attack had failed completely.

It was now little more than 15 minutes since the initial landings. Six of the seven primary targets had been eliminated and the observation domes facing Maastricht blinded. Swastika flags were now draped over five gun emplacements: Maastricht 1 and 2, Coupole Nord, Mi-Sud, and Mi-Nord, while the MICA position had been overrun as well as two false cupolas destroyed. When the scheduled Stuka support arrived overhead at H+25 (0450hrs), the dive-bombers observed the array of swastikas and began to pound the perimeter defences, in particular Bloc 1 and the administrative buildings, causing severe damage and several casualties. Coupole Sud was also subjected to repeated dive-bombing attacks but without damage. On the fortress roof only Coupole 120 of the primary targets remained unscathed due to the glider of Trupp 2 failing to arrive at Fort Eben Emael. Their secondary target, the triple 75mm gun casemate Visé, was also intact. The last of the nine gliders to land contained Trupp 10 under Oberjäger Huebel, acting as a reserve force as well as carrying the radio team of Jägers Gilg and Kultz. The latter's first task was to contact Leutnant Witzig but in his absence they encountered Feldwebel Wenzel. Realizing that Witzig was missing, Wenzel assumed command of Sturmgruppe Granit as Lt. Delica was stuck inside Maastricht 1 for the time being. Now that the smoke had cleared from inside Mi-Nord, Wenzel set up his command post and first-aid dressing station inside. Once the radio was set up beside Mi-Nord, Wenzel transmitted his first laconic message to Maj. Koch at 0442hrs – 'Target reached. Everything in order.' Soon afterwards, he ordered Huebel to attack Visé 1 as its guns were firing sporadically into the surrounding countryside following explicitly the instructions of the alert – *Attaque générale*. Once more the power of the hollow-charge weapon achieved decisive results when a 12.5kg charge blasted one 75mm gun embrasure causing the gun crew to withdraw to the intermediate level. Although troops returned to the position under the command of Lt. Desloovere and fired some more rounds, the crew left once more when he was ordered to return to the command post.

With no firing now from Visé 1, Trupp 5 took the opportunity to attack Coupole Sud at the southern-most tip of the fortress. At 0535hrs, a 50kg hollow-charge weapon was detonated on the retracted cupola, causing damage to one of the 75mm guns, but the gun crew subsequently repaired this. Thinking that the position had been rendered inoperable, the Germans left and regrouped near the Graindorge with their Belgian prisoners. Shortly before two He111 bombers had dropped containers by parachute with more ammunition and explosives. Belgian POWs were forced to retrieve the containers as Belgian artillery rounds were now impacting on the roof of the fortress. Unbeknownst to Truppe 5 and 8, Coupole 120 was still in Belgian hands. They had no way of

This remarkable photograph shows the view from the German command post of Mi-Nord during the course of the fighting of 10 May, with Belgian artillery shells bursting on the surface of the fortress. To the right is the earth embankment between Mi-Nord and Mi-Sud, with the barbed wire entanglements to its front. In the middle distance is the DFS 230 of Trupp 9, whose primary target was Mi-Sud. In the distance to the left is the DFS 230 of Trupp 1, whose primary target was Maastricht 1, situated in the far background. The white shapes on the ground are the parachutes of the resupply containers. During the course of the battle, the Belgian artillery of the surrounding units and the forts to the south, Barchon, Evegnée and Pontisse, fired some 2,200 shells onto Fort Eben Emael. Sheltered in their captured casemates, the barrage had little but nuisance effect on Sturmgruppe Granit, and the Belgian artillery would have been better served by bombarding German units attempting to cross the Meuse River and Albert Canal. This photograph was taken by Helmut Wenzel, who normally went into action with a pair of binoculars and a camera around his neck. (Fort Eben Emael)

During the morning of 11 May, Oberleutnant Witzig kept the garrison off-guard by repeatedly setting off explosive charges that reverberated throughout the fortress and further demoralized the Belgian defenders. The most devastating of these occurred at 0850hrs when a 50kg charge was detonated against the armoured doors of Maastricht 1 on the intermediate level. The massive explosion blew off the internal door, killing six Belgian soldiers and wounding several others. The dead were privates Corombelle, Dujardin, Gillet, Lebeau, Martin and Massotte. The blast wave funnelled down the tunnels and galleries, causing barrels of calcium chloride stored in the open passageways to burst and exude noxious fumes. The Belgian defenders now believed they were under a gas attack, and were forced to wear gasmasks to combat the fumes. It was another serious blow to an already demoralized garrison. The chaplain's diary continues – 'The bombs are still making the fort shake to its foundations. Maastricht 1 and Mi-Nord are said to have exploded. The wounded keep arriving at the infirmary. Gillet is brought to the infirmary, dying. His face and hands are burnt black … As for Massotte, he is still conscious when they bring him to the infirmary … I administer the extreme unction and together we say the prayers for the dying. He passes away very quietly in front of his comrades.'

knowing that Trupp 2 had been forced down inside Germany when its glider's towrope parted and the gun emplacement remained intact although inoperative. Since the outset of the attack, the gun crew of Coupole 120 had been feverishly trying to bring their powerful 120mm guns into action, but mechanical failures had prevented them from doing so.

The commander of the gun emplacement, Maréchal des logis Cremers, observed them and fired his rifle through the horizontal slot for the telescopic sight that had not been delivered. Unteroffizer Lange, the glider pilot of Trupp 5, and a Belgian soldier, Private Kips, were hit and wounded. With no 50kg charges to hand, the Germans shoved 1kg charges down the barrels and, fortuitously, they detonated at the moment the gun breeches were open, causing blast and flame to burst inside the cupola. As the lights failed, the gun crew retreated to the intermediate level. The remnants of Truppe 5 and 8, the latter now under the command of Oberjäger Else following the death of Oberjäger Unger, made their way to Mi-Nord and reported to Feldwebel Wenzel. As he spoke French, the wounded Lange was put in charge of the Belgian prisoners. The only active Belgian gun emplacement now was Visé 2, which was firing random rounds. However, as it was orientated southwards it was of no concern to Sturmgruppe Granit. In order to maintain pressure on the Belgian defenders, the men of Trupp 3 ventured down the hillside below their primary target, Maastricht 1, and attacked Bloc 2 at the head of the water-filled anti-tank ditch. At 0630hrs, a 50kg charge was placed over the observation dome and detonated, killing Private Decoutry inside. The remainder of the gun crew evacuated the position but returned later. At the same time, the Belgians mounted their first counter-attack from Bloc 1. However, it comprised just one junior officer, two NCOs and ten soldiers. They were armed only with rifles as they had no automatic weapons. As they climbed the slope from Bloc 1, there was a massive explosion as the observation dome of Bloc 2 was demolished and the Belgians withdrew whence they came to the dismay of Maj. Jottrand. A second sortie was made from Bloc 1 around 0800hrs but it also caused no inconvenience to the German attackers.

Beside the fear of Belgian counter-attacks, the major concern for Fw. Wenzel was Coupole 120, the most powerful gun emplacement of Fort Eben Emael. Although damaged by the earlier assault, its guns still dominated the bridges over the Albert Canal to the north. Another attempt to destroy the gun emplacement was made at 0645hrs, when a 50kg charge was detonated above the left-hand 120mm gun. Although there was no penetration of the heavily armoured carapace, the two guns were damaged. Once more Cremers and his team went to work, and by 0800hrs the right-hand 120mm gun was repaired and ready to fire. He and Lt. Dehousse repeatedly sought permission from the command post to fire but got no response. With the bridges across the Meuse River demolished by the Dutch, the whole German Army was stuck on the east bank of the river in an ever-growing expanse of tanks, trucks, and men. Coupole 120 was designed specifically to engage and destroy such targets at long range, but no fire orders were given. Despite his fortress being overrun by Germans, Maj. Jottrand maintained that he was forbidden to fire into Holland. The final opportunity for Fort Eben Emael to redeem itself was lost. To add insult to injury, a German paratrooper was sitting astride one of the 120mm guns in a drunken stupor as the cupola revolved aimlessly. Oberjäger Grechza of Trupp 5 had filled his water canteen with rum prior to the assault. He declaimed that it was purely for administration to the wounded but had obviously forgotten in the heat of the action and consumed it himself. His drunken antics did not amuse Fw. Wenzel, and Grechza was severely reprimanded. Around 0930hrs, the paratroopers finally immobilized Coupole 120 by jamming numerous explosive charges down both barrels. The ensuing explosions damaged the guns beyond repair. At 1000hrs, the command post issued two fire missions to Coupole 120 with one towards Maastricht and one towards Lanaye. It was too little, too late. After inspecting the damaged cupola several times, the Belgian gun crew finally withdrew to the intermediate level around 1400hrs and sealed off the position behind the barrier of steel beams, sandbags and armoured doors. All the primary objectives of Sturmgruppe Granit had been eliminated. Like an ageing lion, Fort Eben Emael was now blind and toothless.

The long lingering death of Fort Eben Emael

For all intents and purposes Sturmgruppe Granit had succeeded in its mission. Their task now was to hold the top of Fort Eben Emael until relieved by the men of Pionierbataillon 51 and Infanterie Regiment 151. This was scheduled for 1100hrs on 10 May 1940, but because of the destroyed bridges over the Meuse River and at Kanne this was not to be. It was going to be a long wait for the men of Sturmgruppe Granit. The following was written by Kurt Engelmann of Trupp 4, whose recollections offer a vivid account of that long, hot day and the death throes of Fort Eben Emael.

> It was around 0830hrs when a lone glider flew over the fort and landed not very far from the northern rampart. In it was Oberleutnant Witzig and Trupp 11, who had been forced to land on a meadow beside the Rhine when the tow rope broke shortly after take-off. In a relatively short time, Witzig was able to organize a replacement Ju52 tow aircraft, which was able to land on the meadow and take-off again with the DFS 230 of Trupp 11. Witzig was quickly briefed by Fw Wenzel and he assumed command of the assault group. In the meantime, it had been established that Maier's Trupp 2 had not landed on the fort. His pilot, Brendenbeck, had been forced to land at Düren near the Dutch border. During the course of the day, Trupp 2 had fought its way to the edge of the fort, but were unable to penetrate the fort's defences, with the result that Casemate 24 [Coupole 120] had not yet been destroyed.
>
> Heinemann's Trupp 7, whose target was an armoured cupola on the northern tip outside the blockade belt and which turned out to be a dummy installation, was unable to join the fighting within the fort. Due to these setbacks and the losses, our fighting strength had been reduced to 60 men, who were facing a force of approximately 600 Belgian soldiers in the fort and casemates. By midday things had quietened down. The sun was beating down and the men were becoming

Specially configured units backed Sturmabteilung Koch in order to provide fire support and reinforcement as soon as possible after the capture of the bridges. The main one was Infanterie Regiment 151, with the attached Pionierbataillon 51. As a motorized formation, it came under 'Marschgruppe Rot' of the 4th Panzer Division, and was at the forefront of the advance. In addition, there was Flakabteilung Aldinger with three heavy and two light Flak batteries. The 88mm Flak guns also gave fire support to the paratroopers, while the light Flak batteries were tasked with providing anti-aircraft defences around the captured bridges against Allied bombers. The men of Pionierbataillon 51 were issued with inflatable assault boats and they were used to cross the Albert Canal below Kanne to link up with Sturmgruppe Granit on the morning of 11 May. The commander of the pioneers, Oberstleutnant Mikosch, actually accepted the surrender of Fort Eben Emael from Maj. Jottrand soon after midday after he had been promised that there were no time delay demolitions in the fortress. (National Archives and Records Administration)

The chaplain's final diary entry reads: 'Captain Vamecq, ordered to negotiate the surrender, heads for the entrance of the fort escorted by a private holding a white flag but the Germans keep firing. A second attempt gets a better result. The firing ceases and negotiations begin. It takes some time before he returns. Unconditional surrender has been demanded. German soldiers approach the fort. The garrison is ordered to lay down their arms and to form ranks four abreast to leave the fort with officers in front. The medical personnel are to stay in the fort with the wounded. They will be looked after later on. While the men get rid of their weapons and form ranks we stay at the cross roads of the underground galleries. I shake hands with all those passing by. Slowly the column leaves the fort, which now becomes silent.' In all, the garrison sustained 21 dead and 61 wounded. Sturmgruppe Granit suffered six fatalities during the assault of Fort Eben Emael, including the death of Oberjäger Maier of Trupp 2 during the fighting around the Kanne bridge. All six were buried at the northernmost tip of the fortress overlooking the Albert Canal beneath a large crucifix. The six dead paratroopers were Oberjäger Max Maier, Oberjäger Willi Hübel, Oberjäger Otto Unger, Obergefreiter Helmuth Bögle, Gefreiter Kurt Jürgensen and Gefreiter Fritz Kruck. The bodies were subsequently moved to the military cemetery at Ysselsteyn in Holland, where they rest to this day.

very thirsty, particularly as everyone had expected to be relieved by this time. A bunker in the southeast of the fort [Coupole Sud] suddenly began shelling our positions on the northern tip with shrapnel rounds, which was repeated at intervals throughout the afternoon.

Heavy gunfire broke out in the south-west of the fort shortly after 1200hrs. Oberleutnant Witzig ordered Feldwebel Wenzel to move up with some men, but they were unable to locate the enemy in the difficult terrain. For a short time we had to take cover in Trupp 3's Casemate 12, as the fire became heavier and heavier. Feldwebel Wenzel was at this time wounded by a bullet, which grazed his head. Several times we had to move against the Belgians in the vicinity of Oberjäger Arendt's Casemate 12 [Maaastricht 1], as fresh troops had been moved up from Wonck. Although we suffered some losses, the Belgians were unable to make a successful coordinated attack. The shooting had stopped in this area after 1700hrs and Feldwebel Wenzel returned to the northern tip with his men. Oberleutnant Witzig deployed his further depleted Trupp to the defensive position at the northern rampart, particularly as it was becoming dark and it was uncertain whether the Belgians would launch a counter-attack on the fort. All of us were extremely nervous in the dark, everyone stared into the darkness with their weapons at the ready, expecting an attack at any minute. Some artillery began firing at about 2100hrs, but we were lucky and did not suffer any further losses.

Casemate 17 [Canal Nord], a bunker in the canal wall, illuminated the canal with its searchlights and had successfully prevented the army pioneers from crossing until then. During the afternoon, Oberleutnant Witzig had already seen how dangerous this position was and sent Oberjäger Harlos and Trupp 6 to tackle it. On three occasions, charges were lowered on a rope and detonated beside the bunker, but its 60mm gun continued to fire. In the north-east we frequently saw flares, which encouraged us to believe that the army was not very far away. In spite of this, the night seemed endless, particularly as the artillery fire also kept flaring up against us.

Finally dawn approached and it seemed to us like a miracle that the Belgians had not launched a counter-attack and that we had survived the night. At around 0500hrs on 11 May, 1 Zug of Pionierbataillon 51 under the command of Oberfeldwebel Portsteffen, had fought its way to the fort. We were glad to see that German relief forces were finally close. It began to get light and our mood picked up again, we became aware of our hunger and above all, our thirst. We suddenly came under fire again from Casemate 23 [Coupole Sud] and from the northern tip we were able to watch two German anti-tank guns duelling with Casemate 17 [Canal Nord] on the canal wall. The shells fired from the canal bunker hit the village and church at Kanne, but after a short time it was finally knocked out.

Time passed very slowly and we kept on hearing shots from the uncleared area in the south-east, but there was no enemy to be seen. At 1215hrs, the fort was finally handed over to Oberstleutnant Mikosch by the fort commander, Major Jottrand. The garrison of almost 1,000 men began the trek into captivity. Our assault group had suffered 6 dead and 18 wounded. Belgian casualties were 21 dead and 61 wounded [sic]. After burying the dead at the fort, we marched away, with some of our wounded having to be carried on improvised stretchers. This turned into a problem between the bushes and trees on the steep ground leading to the entrance position, particularly as some shooting broke out, which was apparently caused by some of the army pioneers.

We finally reached the entrance position and were able to take a short break. Some men rushed into the destroyed village [Eben Emael], searched a bar and found the water that we had been longing for. We quickly quenched our thirst and took as much as we could for our wounded and other comrades. We continued along the canal with the wounded transported some of the way on inflatable boats. We became soaked when we had to wade part of the way through the floods. We were then attacked by French bombers and since there was no cover we had to throw ourselves flat on the ground. Fortunately for us the bombs fell into the water about 40m away from us. We then continued towards the village of Kanne, where we handed our wounded over to the medics at the dressing station.

Our march then continued to Maastricht, which took us two hours. We spent the night on the floor between the classroom benches in a local school, where we were unable to forget the sounds of screaming shells and gunfire. On 12 May, we received our first cup of coffee, what a pleasure! It was only then did we realize that it was Whitsun. Our trucks turned up at around midday and we set off towards the Meuse bridge. There we had to withstand an attack by some 20 British bombers before our journey could continue. At around 1700hrs we reached Köln-Dellenbrück and after a short break we continued on to Köln-Ostheim, where a large reception and medal award ceremony awaited us. On 13 May, we continued on our journey to Münster, where another reception was held in our honour. This time we were awarded the Iron Cross 1st Class by General Kesselring. This was followed by a well-earned 14-day leave, which helped us to forget the hardships we had endured at Eben Emael.

After the battle for Fort Eben Emael and the Albert Canal bridges, the paratroopers of Sturmabteilung Koch were feted as heroes in the German press, and many of them featured on postcards such as this one of Leutnant Egon Delica, the air liaison officer. The illustration shows Lt. Delica in the distinctive paratrooper's smock and helmet, as well as the Ritterkreuz he received from the hands of Adolf Hitler on 16 May 1940. Over his shoulders are representations of Fort Eben Emael, including Coupole 120 and the Caster cutting. At top left is the insignia of the 7th Flieger Division, the parent organisation of Sturmabteilung Koch. It is curious that Lt. Delica landed with Trupp 1 when the only radio and its operators were with Trupp 10. For much of the battle, Lt. Delica sheltered inside the casemate Maastricht 1 while the radio was with Fw. Wenzel at Mi-Nord. The latter coordinated Luftwaffe air support and communicated with the forward headquarters of Sturmabteilung Koch although, as an officer, Lt. Delica was of a superior rank and Oberleutnant Witzig's nominal deputy.

Because of his drunken antics on Coupole 120, Oberjäger Ernst Grechza of Trupp 5 was the only member of Sturmgruppe Granit not to be awarded the Iron Cross 1st Class; his was only 2nd Class. In addition, the two soldiers sentenced to death for their earlier lapse of security were reprieved after the success of the operation and resumed their duties as paratroopers. All of the officers of Sturmabteilung Koch, beside those injured, received the Ritterkreuz (Knight's Cross of the Iron Cross) from Adolf Hitler on 16 May at the Führerhauptquartier 'Felsennest', 50km south-west of Bonn. The casualty list for Sturmgruppe Granit was six dead and 18 wounded during the assault on Fort Eben Emael, including those of Trupp 2. The Belgian defenders of the fort suffered 21 dead and 61 injured. This total does not include those attached to the garrison or any of the infantry units that mounted counter-attacks against the fort. The total casualties of Sturmabteilung Koch were 43 dead, 100 wounded and one missing in action. The latter was a member of Sturmgruppe Eisen who was captured and later released at Dunkirk. The men of the motorized units sent to relieve Sturmabteilung Koch suffered 12 dead, 61 wounded, and two missing in action. Thus, the grand total of casualties in the operation to capture the bridges over the Albert Canal and the elimination of Fort Eben Emael was 55 dead, 161 wounded and three missing in action. The Belgian losses were considerably higher. Nevertheless, it was a remarkably low price to pay for such a high strategic prize. The heartland of Belgium was now laid open to the panzers of the German Sixth Army.

Blame and counterblame

The fall of Fort Eben Emael was a disaster for the Allies. *Fall Gelb* now unfolded with Teutonic precision. Holland collapsed within five days. Belgium capitulated on 28 May with the last fort of the *Position Fortifiée de Liège* at Tancrémont surrendering the next day. France fell on 25 June following a 42-day blitzkrieg campaign that stunned the world. The British Expeditionary Force limped home from Dunkirk devoid of tanks and heavy weapons. Hitler was now master of Europe from the Atlantic Ocean to the Bug River in Poland, and the key to that stupendous victory was a Belgian fortress near the village of Eben Emael. Once hailed as the strongest fortress in the world and deemed to be impregnable, Fort Eben Emael surrendered after just 30 hours, although it was effectively subdued within the first 30 minutes. This was achieved by a fighting force of 85 pioneers and pilots. It was, and remains, one of the most remarkable feats of arms in the history of warfare. Total operational secrecy and the use of innovative technological weapons were decisive to success. But crucially, a senior non-commissioned officer, Feldwebel Helmut Wenzel, commanded this devastating attack during the critical opening phase in the absence of his commanding officer. It was an outstanding example of *Auftragstaktik* – the leadership principle practised by the German armed forces for the past 200 years[5]. This is based on trusting the skills and commitment of subordinates to perform their duties to the utmost in the execution of an agreed operational plan as defined by a commander, who also provides the necessary resources to undertake the task. The men of Sturmgruppe Granit were provided with the means through the use of assault gliders and hollow charge weapons, which were both employed for the first time in warfare. The pioneers also underwent superlative training, and the end result was a unit with supreme morale.

The Belgian defenders of Fort Eben Emael by comparison did not, and neither did the Belgian field army in the surrounding countryside. The 4e Division

Pioneers of Trupp 4 pose for a photograph after the surrender of Fort Eben Emael with, from left to right: Karl Polzin, Eddi Schmidt, Helmut Wenzel, Otto Bräutigam (glider pilot), Fritz Florian, and Kurt Engelmann. The latter's dramatic account of the battle features in the text. The success of Sturmgruppe Granit was fundamentally due to the calibre of men such as these. Superbly trained and highly motivated, they were the living proof of Napoleon's dictum that 'Morale is to the materiel by a factor of three to one'. Although the Belgians made many grave errors in the defence of Fort Eben Emael, nothing can detract from the courage and military prowess of the pioneers of Sturmgruppe Granit in the first glider-borne assault in history, and much of that success was down to one man, Feldwebel Helmut Wenzel. Otto Bräutigam was killed in 1941 whilst flying a Gigant glider. Karl Polzin also died in 1941 in a friendly fire incident. The rest survived the war. (Fort Eben Emael)

[5] *Auftragstaktik* was the pre-eminent command and control principle of the Wehrmacht and remains so to this day in the Bundeswehr. In 1998, *Auftragstaktik* was codified once more as doctrine in Germany Army Regulation AR 100/100, 'Command and Control in Battle'.

d'Infanterie of I Corps to the north of the fortress in the area of Veldwezelt was acknowledged to be the worst in the Belgian army and its men surrendered wholesale without fighting, thus compromising the flanking formations. Other units fought valiantly, such as the 2e Carabiniers against the bridgehead of Sturmgruppe Beton at Vroenhoven. The defenders of Fort Eben Emael fought stubbornly, but they were ill-served by their officers. Troop morale is a prime responsibility for officers and commanders of all ranks and specialities, be they infantry or artillery. It was apparent that the calibre of the officers of Fort Eben Emael was deficient, with too many inexperienced reservists. This manifested itself in defective equipment, inadequate training, poor operating procedures, lack of recreational facilities – indeed the list goes on. Whereas flexibility was inculcated into the German soldier through *Auftragstaktik*, none was expected of the Belgian soldier, and the officers or senior NCOs displayed little. In fact, initiative was actively discouraged. On those occasions that Maj. Jottrand did actually suggest improvements or modifications to the defences of Fort Eben Emael, such as barbed wire around the gun casemates, he was invariably dismissed out of hand by higher command.

The officers of Sturmabteilung Koch being presented the Ritterkreuz for their part in the assaults on Eben Emael and the bridges over the Albert Canal on 10 May 1940. The photo was taken on 16 May at Führerhauptquartier 'Felsennest', 50km south-west of Bonn. From left to right: Hauptmann Walter Koch, Oberleutnant Rudolf Witzig, Oberleutnant Gustav Altmann. Other officers present are: Oberleutnant Otto Zierach, Oberarzt Dr. Rolf Jäger, Leutnant Egon Delica, Leutnant Helmut Ringler, Leutnant Joachim Meissner, Leutnant Gerhard Schacht. Not present was Leutnant Martin Schächter, who remained in hospital after being wounded during the fierce fighting at Kanne.

Fort Eben Emael was designed to withstand attack from all quarters, and that included from above. The four machine guns of the MICA position were more than sufficient to engage and destroy nine fabric-covered gliders in the air. Any that survived to land on the fortress were sitting targets for the concerted firepower of four multiple 75mm guns and two multiple machine-gun emplacements. Automatic fire from Mi-Nord and Mi-Sud, combined with canister rounds from ten 75mm guns, could, and should, have swept Sturmgruppe Granit off the face of the earth within moments of landing. That not a single one of these gun emplacements engaged the enemy is an appalling indictment of the level of readiness of the garrison and its leadership. The failure to open ammunition boxes, the incorrect alert given of *Attaque générale* rather than *Attaque massif*, the inability to fire the general alert in time to summon reserves, and the lack of canister rounds to hand were all the fault of the garrison's officers. These were exacerbated by Maj. Jottrand's determination to empty and demolish the two administrative buildings outside Bloc 1. The tactical importance of this requirement was so marginal as to defy belief, and to strip the principal gun emplacements of their crews, as well as the observers on top of the fortress, to undertake this task was totally reprehensible. These were the actions of an unimaginative and methodical officer given to following orders without question. But all the blame cannot be laid at the door of Maj. Jottrand, although this is exactly what happened in the post-war inquiry initiated by the Belgian Government.

Belgium was liberated in early 1945 after five years of bitter occupation by the Nazis. During that time the garrison had been prisoners of war in a camp at Fallingbostel in Germany; for the first six months in total isolation because of their possible knowledge of hollow-charge weapons. Many officers and men

During the war, the Germans used Fort Eben Emael as a barracks and storage facility. Five of the six electrical generators were removed and used in fortifications of the Atlantic Wall. This photograph was taken in 1944 and shows the tree line now obscuring the air ventilation outlet. After four years of occupation, Fort Eben Emael was captured by the US 30th Infantry Division on 10 September 1944 without a struggle. The Germans made no attempt to repair the guns or their emplacements, so much of the site remains as it was immediately after their original assault in 1940.

wrote detailed accounts of the fall of Fort Eben Emael, but these were suppressed in the subsequent inquiry. As the war ended, Belgium suffered a constitutional crisis and its economy was in tatters. There was little appetite for exposing the failings of the political and military establishments through a thorough and open investigation. It was simpler to blame the garrison and allow spurious stories of spies and sabotage to circulate. However, the real blame lay with the body politic and in particular in the mental lethargy of the Belgian High Command. After many years of deliberation dating back to 1890, Fort Eben Emael finally became operational in 1935. At a cost of approximately 250 million Belgian Francs, its construction consumed a significant proportion of the Belgian defence budget. As its strategic position was so vital to the national defence of the country, it was incumbent upon the Belgian High Command to maintain the fortress at the highest level of preparedness and efficiency. Under the dynamic leadership of its first commander, Major Decoux, Fort Eben Emael was a formidable military installation as originally configured. But any institution required constant review and improvement if it was to prosper but this did not happen because of a hidebound higher command. Major Decoux was replaced by a reluctant, ageing major in June 1939 when more dynamic leadership was required with the prospect of war looming. This was the fault of higher command, as was the appointment of inexperienced reserve officers and insufficient manpower for the garrison. Few improvements were made to the fortress prior to 1940, and its operational efficiency diminished as the garrison's morale declined.

FORT EBEN-EMAEL

FORT FEE A.S.B.L. EBEN-EMAEL

En 1940, fleuron des forts de Liège et réputé imprenable. Aujourd'hui, un musée, un lieu d'histoire et de mémoire

In 1940, de bloem van de forten van Luik en oninneembaar. Vandaag, een historisch museum en een herinnering plaats

Fort Eben Emael remains a Belgian army installation to this day and is subject to military law. It was not until 1986 that the general public was allowed to visit the site. The association 'Fort Eben Emael' – FEE – was founded to preserve the memory and the fabric of the fortress. FEE was recognized by the military authorities on 15 January 1988, and thereafter the association has conducted guided tours for the public. However, these are limited to a very specific number of weekends in the year, unless a special visit is arranged in advance. Since 1988, FEE with the assistance of the Belgian Ministry of Defence has refurbished some of the interior rooms and gun emplacements. There is also a museum containing many artefacts of the period. A guided tour of the fortress interior takes approximately two hours, and the dates for the weekend visits are posted on the internet. For further information, consult www.fort-eben-emael.be
(Courtesy Fort Eben Emael)

Despite these problems, Fort Eben Emael remained a powerful entity with an awesome reputation of impregnability. There is no doubt that further measures should have been implemented to bolster that reputation. The simple expedient of installing lengths of scrap railway lines vertically in the top surface of the fortress would have forestalled any attack by gliders at a cost of a few thousand Belgian Francs. But the mindset of the Belgian High Command remained embedded in World War I with its overriding concept of static linear defence. This led to their greatest failure by implementing the overly complex system of command and control, whereby the individual gunemplacements of Fort Eben Emael were directed by other units outside the fortress with neither the means of communications to do so nor the intelligence to implement any effective fire missions. The situation became so arcane that the garrison commander did not have the authority to fire any of his main artillery weapons. This was compounded by the proscription to fire any guns into or over Dutch territory. These factors alone effectively emasculated Fort Eben Emael, but the Belgian High Command was further to blame in its failure to heed the threat of imminent invasion by the Germans and issue a timely alert to the field army and defensive forts. Once belatedly declared, the high command remained incommunicado for several critical hours as it moved to its wartime field headquarters. It was a recipe for disaster that unfolded with an awful inevitability. Fort Eben Emael was conceived in political turmoil, it died through incompetent military management, and was buried in recrimination, literally and figuratively, in the empty underground tunnels, galleries and shattered gun emplacements of the fortress. For a generation it remained a closed military secret. In the words of the great French writer Victor Hugo: 'On résiste à l'invasion des armées; on ne résiste pas à l'invasion des idées.' The Belgian High Command and political establishment failed on both counts. It was the soldiers and citizens of Belgium that paid the price for their failure.

After many years of neglect, the interior of Fort Eben Emael is gradually being refurbished as part of a public museum. This shows the NCOs' sleeping quarters in the main underground accommodation area of the *Caserne Souterraine*.

The Fort Eben Emael of today is much different from the fortress of May 1940. With over 60 years of growth, much of the terrain is overgrown with mature trees and vegetation, while the top surface is now farmland. This view shows the top of Coupole Nord looking southwards to Coupole Sud. Between the two gun emplacements were the MICA anti-aircraft position and, to the right, the Graindorge barracks. The DFS 230 gliders made their final approach from the south, sweeping low over Coupole Sud, with those of Truppe 5 and 8 landing in the foreground close to Coupole Nord. The detonation points of the two 50kg hollow-charge weapons are visible on Coupole Nord and, interestingly, it is possible to see the pattern of the camouflage netting fused into the steel by the heat of the explosions.

Organization of Sturmgruppe Granit

The squads are shown with their primary targets and their breakdown into officers, NCOs and enlisted men: thus 1:2:5 signifies one officer, two NCOs, and five enlisted men. There was one squad (Trupp) per glider and the name of the squad leader (Truppführer) appears first, followed by the glider pilot. Sturmgruppe Granit comprised 11 gliders with a total of 85 personnel. They were armed with six machine guns, 18 sub-machine guns, 54 rifles and 85 pistols, plus a total of 30,000 rounds of ammunition. There were also 2,401kg of explosive devices, four flamethrowers, five signal pistols, various types of hand grenades, seven ladders, 13 Nazi flags, 71 other tools and one radio set. The parentheses indicate either the specialized role or the casualties of Sturmgruppe Granit incurred at Fort Eben Emael, while the brackets indicate the fate of the troops during the war.

Trupp1 EBEN 3 and Maastricht 2 – 1:2:5
Hans Niedermeier
Gerhard Raschke
Egon Delica – (Air liaison officer)
Heinrich List – [KIA 1942 Russia]
Richard Drucks – [KIA 1944 Italy]
Willi Krämer
Peter Gräf
Wilhelm Stucke – [KIA 1941 Crete]

Trupp 2 Coupole 120 – 0:3:5
Max Maier – (KIA EE)
Bredenbeck – [KIA 1944 Jugoslavia]
Walter Meier – (WIA EE)
Gerhard Iskra – [KIA 1943 Tunisia]
Wilhelm Ölmann – [KIA 1941 Crete]
Fritz Gehlich – [KIA 1944 Russia]
Paul Bader – (WIA EE) [KIA 1942 Tunisia]
Hans Comdür – [KIA 1941 Crete]

Trupp 3 Maastricht 1 – 0:2:5
Peter Arendt [Died 3.12.1942]
Alfred Supper
Gustav Merz – (WIA EE) [KIA 1941 Crete]
Josef Müller – [KIA 1941 Crete]
Paul Kupsch
Helmut Stopp – [Fate unknown]
Erwin Franz

Trupp 4 EBEN 2 and Mi-Nord – 0:2:6
Helmut Wenzel – (WIA EE)
Otto Bräutigam – [KIA 1941]
Karl Polzin – [KIA 1941]
Eddi Schmidt
Fritz Köhler
Fritz Florian
Kurt Engelmann
Windemuth – (WIA EE) [Fate unknown]

Trupp 5 MICA anti-aircraft position – 0:3:5
Erwin Haug
Heiner Lange – (WIA EE)
Ernst Grechza – [KIA 1941 Crete]
Franz Jannowski – (WIA EE)
Egon Hartmann – (WIA EE)
Rudolf Stützinger – [KIA 1941 Crete]
Helmuth Bögle – (KIA EE)
Gerhard Becker

Trupp 6 False cupola at northern end of fortress – 0:3:5
Harlos – [KIA 1941 Crete]
Ziller – [KIA 1945]
Werner Grams – [Fate unknown]
Peter Zirwes – [KIA 1942 Russia]
Hans Grigowski
Franz Lukascheck
Richard Bläser
Walter Kippnick

Trupp 7 False cupola at northern end of fortress – 0:2:6
Fritz Heinemann
Heinz Scheithauer – (WIA EE)
Aloys Passman – (WIA EE) [KIA 1941 Crete]
Michalke – (WIA EE) [Fate unknown]
Harm Mülder

Wolfgang Schultz
Wilhelm Höpfner – (WIA EE)
Wilhelm Alefs

Trupp 8 Coupole Nord – 0:3:5
Otto Unger – (KIA EE)
Hans Distelmeier
Johannes Else – (WIA EE) [Fate unknown]
Ernst Hierländer – [KIA 1944 Italy]
Kajetan Mayr – (WIA EE)
Bruno Hooge – (WIA) [Fate unknown]
Herbert Plietz – [KIA 1941 Crete]
Heinz Weinert – [KIA Russia]

Trupp 9 Mi-Sud – 0:3:4
Ewald Neuhaus
Günter Schulz – [KIA 1941 Crete]
Ernst Schlosser – (WIA EE)
Wingers
Rolf Jakob – (WIA EE)

Johann Körner – [Fate unknown]
Anton Seltmann – [KIA 1941 Crete]
Hans Braun – [KIA 1941 Crete]

Trupp 10 Reserve – 0:3:5
Willi Hübel – (KIA EE)
Erwin Kraft – [KIA Russia]
Werner Guthan
Bansimir – [Fate unknown]
Kurt Jürgensen – (KIA EE)
Hubert Hansing – [1941 Crete]
Leopold Gilg – (radio operator)
Paul Kautz – (radio operator)

Trupp 11 Reserve – 1:2:4
Fritz Schwarz
Karl Pilz
Uwe Johnsen
Rudolf Witzig
Fritz Kruck – (KIA EE)
Hans-Peter Krenz
Otto Braun – (WIA EE)

Bibliography

Bikar A., 'Pourquoi le Fort d'Eben Emael est-il tombé si vite?', *Revue Belge d'Histoire Militaire*, XXXI-3/4 Sept–Dec 1995
Lecluse, Henri, *Ceux du Fort d'Eben Emael*, Amicale du Fort d'Eben Emael, 1995
McRaven, William H., *Special Operations: Case Studies in Special Operations Warfare – Theory and Practice*, Presidio Press, 1990
Mrazek, James E. Jr., *The Fall of Eben Emael*, Presidio Press, 1970
Thonus, Joseph, *La Charge Creuse: L'Arme Inattendue du Plan Jaune Contre Eben Emael*, Centre Liègeois d'Histoire et d'Archeologie Militaires, 1998
Vliegen, René, *Fort Eben Emael*, FEE, 1993

Index

Figures in bold refer to illustrations

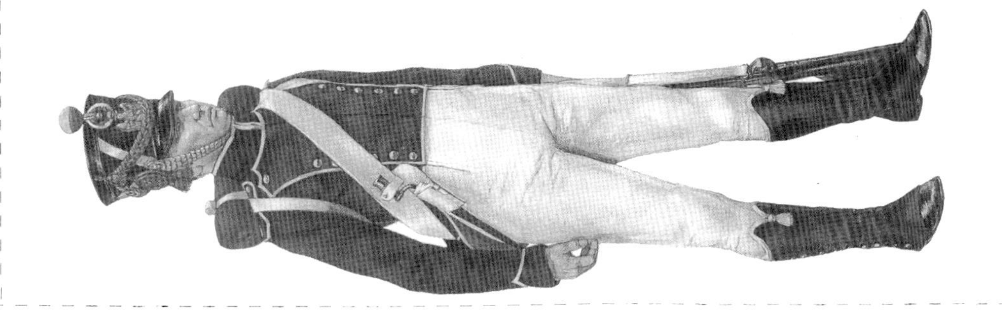

FIND OUT MORE ABOUT OSPREY

❑ Please send me the latest listing of Osprey's publications

❑ I would like to subscribe to Osprey's e-mail newsletter

Title / rank

Name

Address

City / county

Postcode / zip state / country

e-mail

FOR

I am interested in:

❑ Ancient world
❑ Medieval world
❑ 16th century
❑ 17th century
❑ 18th century
❑ Napoleonic
❑ 19th century
❑ American Civil War
❑ World War 1
❑ World War 2
❑ Modern warfare
❑ Military aviation
❑ Naval warfare

Please send to:

North America:
Osprey Direct , 2427 Bond Street, University Park, IL 60466, USA

UK, Europe and rest of world:
Osprey Direct UK, P.O. Box 140, Wellingborough, Northants, NN8 2FA, United Kingdom

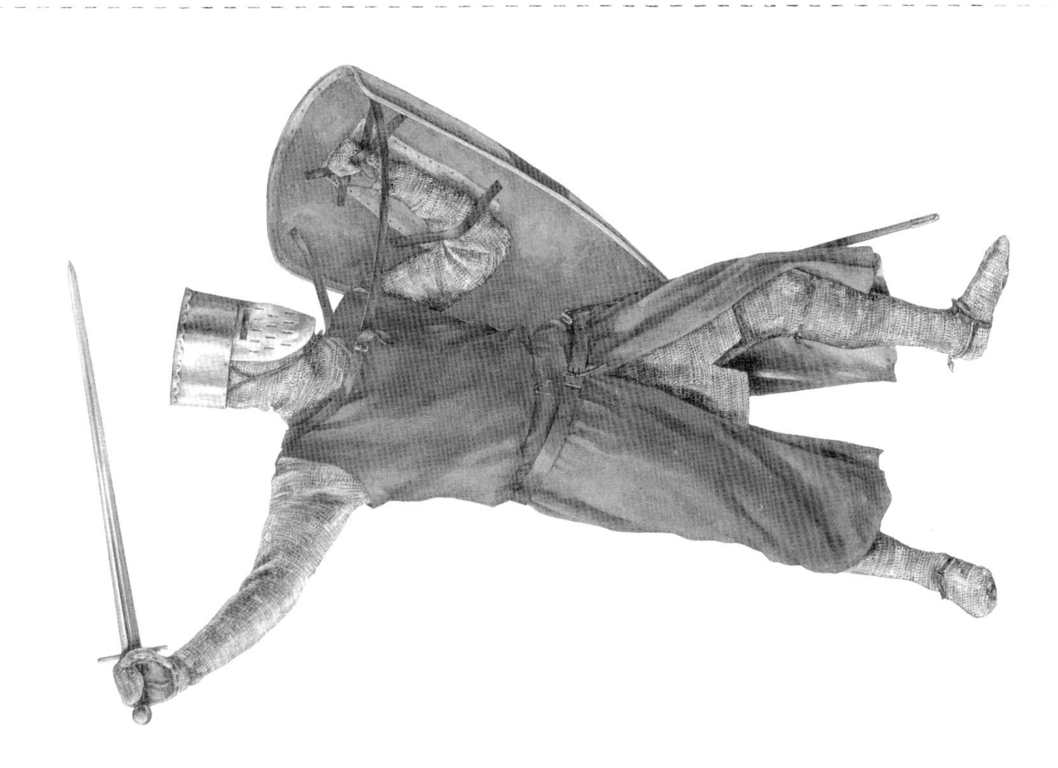

Young Guardsman
Figure taken from *Warrior 22: Imperial Guardsman 1799–1815*
Published by Osprey
Illustrated by Richard Hook

Knight, c.1190
Figure taken from *Warrior 1: Norman Knight 950 – 1204 AD*
Published by Osprey
Illustrated by Christa Hook

POSTCARD